AMERICAN
HERITAGE

June, 1973 • Volume XXIV, Number 4

As dramatists from Aeschylus to O'Neill remind us, psychological flaws are what make characters interesting, and this is equally true when it comes to history. Sometimes physical flaws make a great difference, too—witness the article in this issue about F.D.R.'s handicap. And even flaws in inanimate things can enormously affect our interest in them and consequently their place in history. The crack seen in the photograph above rivals the San Andreas Fault in the amount of attention it has received from concerned Americans. If you have not already recognized it (it is *not* part of the surface of the moon or of Mount Rushmore), you can turn to the last page of this magazine to discover what it is, and when and why this famous fault came into being.

2

AMERICAN HERITAGE

The Magazine of History

EDITOR
Oliver Jensen

ARTICLES EDITOR: E. M. Halliday
EXECUTIVE EDITOR: Nat Brandt
ASSOCIATE EDITOR: Barbara Klaw
ART DIRECTOR: Emma Landau
ASSISTANT EDITOR: Richard F. Snow

PICTURE EDITORS
Carla Davidson   Mary Dawn Earley
ASSISTANT: Devorah K. Cohen

COPY EDITOR
Joyce O'Connor
ASSOCIATE COPY EDITOR: Anne D. Steinhardt

EDITORIAL ASSISTANTS
Anne Anderson   Carolyn Jones

CONSULTING EDITOR: Joan Paterson Kerr

CONTRIBUTING EDITORS
Robert C. Alberts   Robert S. Gallagher
Richard M. Ketchum   Bernard A. Weisberger

ADVISORY BOARD
Carl Carmer   Eric F. Goldman
Gerald Carson   Louis C. Jones
Henry Steele Commager   Alvin M. Josephy, Jr.
Marshall B. Davidson   Howard H. Peckham
John A. Garraty   Francis S. Ronalds
S. K. Stevens

AMERICAN HERITAGE PUBLISHING CO., INC.

PRESIDENT AND PUBLISHER
Paul Gottlieb
EDITOR IN CHIEF
Joseph J. Thorndike
SENIOR EDITOR
Bruce Catton
EDITORIAL ART DIRECTOR
Murray Belsky

AMERICAN HERITAGE is published every two months by American Heritage Publishing Co., Inc.; editorial and executive offices, 1221 Ave. of the Americas, New York, N.Y. 10020. Treasurer, Marjorie C. Dyer; Secretary, John C. Taylor III. Correspondence about subscriptions should be sent to American Heritage Subscription Office, 383 West Center St., Marion, Ohio 43302. Single copies: $5. Annual subscriptions: $20 in U.S. and Canada; $21 elsewhere. A ten-year Index covering Volumes VI–XV is available at $5 and a five-year Index of Volumes XVI–XX at $5.

AMERICAN HERITAGE considers but assumes no responsibility for unsolicited materials; these require return postage. Title registered U.S. Patent Office. Second-class postage paid at New York, N.Y., and at additional mailing offices.

Sponsored by
American Association for State & Local History · Society of American Historians

CONTENTS *June, 1973* • *Volume XXIV, Number 4*

COVER: This elegant sewing machine—now the property of the Smithsonian Institution—was submitted to the Patent Office in 1858 by an inventor named James Perry. Oddly enough, Perry was not interested in patenting the graceful horse design, but rather the collection of gears and springs behind it. Inventors were required to submit models with their patent applications for most of the last century. The interesting and occasionally splendid products of this stipulation can be seen in our portfolio beginning on page 49. *Back cover:* The New York City policeman has always had a tough job, but this adulatory 1879 lithograph, now in the Museum of the City of New York, suggests that there may have been more compensations a century ago. The vignettes at the bottom show him hard at work, and above he poses in what appears to be a crime-free area.

THE CHOCOLATE CAMELOT

Three in one: a composite photograph of Milton S. Hershey taken in Nice, France, in 1910. At right is a lamppost at the very heart of the confectioner's utopia. The signs unabashedly designate two of the first streets that were laid out when the town was founded in 1903.

ONCE UPON A TIME A SHY BUT PERSISTENT CANDYMAKER

NAMED HERSHEY DREAMED OF BUILDING HIS OWN UTOPIA . . .

Milton Snavely Hershey, the chocolate man, was talking to an old friend some forty years ago about the strange, artificial, moneymaking town that he had started from scratch, and named for himself, back at the turn of the century: "We haven't any politics, and our employes don't have to live here if they don't want to." He explained how the town of Hershey, set in the lush, rolling dairy land of central Pennsylvania, was run: "When a street is to be paved, or something is required to be done in this town, somebody always notices the need before it becomes imperative. If he happens to be passing our offices, he walks in and tells us, or else he passes the word along through a third party. I am informed, if I am in town, and we go ahead with the work." It was "M.S."—as Hershey was deferentially called—who personally decided what work did or did not need doing, and it was M.S. who paid for it.

"You might liken this business to a large farm," he said, "and when I speak of the business I include the community. We can all find plenty to do without wasting time on rules and regulations. It has been my experience that the expectation of trouble is often one of the chief causes of it. Men make regulations to prevent other men from doing something wrong or foolish. Later it is discovered that the regulation interferes with actions which might be of general benefit. We simply try not to interfere with people who want to work." Hershey deeply resented any criticism of his altruism. A *Fortune* reporter in 1934 claimed that local Pennsylvania Dutch farmers called the characteristic smell in the Hershey air "da chockle shtink," and he continued: "The moral atmosphere of the town is pervaded by another odor —the sweet and oppressive odor of charity." Hershey retorted: "I've always half suspected that some of these so-called New York wonder workers are disgruntled because they can't get their fingers on my money! I've tried to build a town where people can live contentedly, and where they can be happy at work, and where they can live in pleasant surroundings. You'd think I'd get a little credit for what I have done, wouldn't you?"

By the time Hershey died in 1945, at the age of eighty-eight, he had done a great deal. Besides the world's biggest chocolate factory and a trust fund of eighty million dollars, he had created the world's richest orphanage, two hotels including a huge resort, an airport, a lumber company, a department store, a drugstore, a cafeteria, a professional hockey

By ROY BONGARTZ

Right: Hershey's resolute mother, Fanny, in a rare photo. Below: father Henry, a perennial failure.

In a car bursting with friends, Hershey in 1913 celebrated the tenth anniversary of his town. He sits next to his chauffeur, Max. At the far left, holding the American flag, is his wife, Kitty.

High Point, Hershey's twenty-room mansion, was within eyeshot of his factory's smokestacks. It is now used for school social events.

team, a sports arena, a stadium, four golf courses, a soap division, a cold-storage plant, a slaughterhouse, a laundry and dry-cleaning business, an elaborate zoo, an amusement park, a greenhouse and nursery, a feed mill, a garden with 120,000 plants in it, a campground, a bakery, a community center, a theatre, a dairy, a monorail, a museum, a coal business, an auto garage, a fertilizer plant, a real-estate operation, and a bank—all in Hershey. There were also, down in Cuba, some sugar mills and a 287-mile-long railroad. After a series of business failures in his twenties and thirties, there was a special sweetness for Hershey in his nearly untroubled triumphs during his middle years as his plant and his town prospered. But there was bitterness again toward the end of his life as the world began to play tricks on him, to change around him, to refuse to give thanks to him any more. Hershey's story spans two worlds. When he first began selling candy, the industrial revolution had only just come into full bloom; machines and the "progress" they would bring were beloved and honored on all sides. When he finally quit any active role in his business, a few months before he died, another world war had killed the notion of "progress" and robbed the machine of its old aura of do-gooder. Somehow the times had robbed Hershey of his do-gooder mantle as well. The younger workers in his plant were demanding a share of the country's wealth as their right, not as a gift of M. S. Hershey. But the old man never quite figured out these new people.

Hershey's great-great-great-great-grandfather, Christian Hershey, immigrated to Pennsylvania from Switzerland in 1709; Milton was born near Hockersville, Pennsylvania—a few miles from the site of present-day Hershey—in 1857. His father, Henry, was a tall, garrulous, restless farmer always experimenting with new crops or improved breeds of poultry and livestock. A freethinker, he never got along with his morally strict and penny-pinching Mennonite wife, Fanny. Henry often left home for months at a time, involved in one or another of some seventeen different trades, at all of which he failed—steelworker, gold miner, fruit-tree expert, and preacher among them. Henry at one time painted still-life pictures in oil for sale locally but sold none, mainly because the religious Plain People of the area forbade any such frivolous, worldly decorations on their walls. Henry was always in the wrong place at the wrong time—he even managed to run a likely product called the Celebrated H. H. Hershey's Cough Drops into the ground just as the famous Smith brothers were beginning to build their fortune. For a long time it seemed as if Milton was following in his father's footsteps, but eventually, with the encouragement and financial help of his mother and her maiden sister—not to say their bossy pushing—he made it in the candy business.

Devotees of great moments in industry may draw in their breath in fearful contemplation of the losses the world might have sustained if Milton's first job had worked out better for him—he was hired as printer's devil on a pacifist newspaper in Millwood Gap called *Der Waffenlose Waechter* (it was bilingual). Thumb-fingered Milton spilled a lot of the type, and, as he later told a biographer, "I lost my job when I let my old straw hat fall on the form rollers—which I may have done on purpose." His mother promptly apprenticed him to a Lancaster confectioner, Joseph H. Royer, who, on Fanny's insistence, soon promoted the young Hershey from handle man on the ice-cream freezer to the candy kitchen, where he might learn something. One night when he left the kitchen, he forgot to turn off the blower on the peanut roaster, so that the street outside was soon filled with burnt peanut shells. But he stayed on, and in the summer of 1876, when he was nineteen, his mother and aunt decided he should quit and go into business for himself in Philadelphia. Aunt Mattie kicked in a hundred fifty dollars to help out and offered to take him to the big city and find him a place.

Mattie found him a storefront at 935 Spring Garden Street and returned to Lancaster, temporarily leaving Milton to his own devices. He boiled up penny candy in the cellar and peddled it by day, but there was no profit in it. He tried to improve business by having fancy four-color cards printed up, with the legend "M. S. HERSHEY, DEALER IN FINE CONFECTIONERY, FRUITS, NUTS, &C." circling a picture of a magnificent building labelled "length 1402 feet width 360 feet," but upon close scrutiny the building turned out to be Machinery Hall at the Philadelphia Centennial Exposition of 1876 rather than the Hershey plant. Meanwhile his mother had to move to Philadelphia and open a boarding house to keep him afloat. Mattie also helped by donating her savings to Milton's business, and when this wasn't enough, she borrowed more money from her brother Abraham and finally moved to Philadelphia too, where she and Fanny spent their evenings wrapping bits of taffy called French Secrets that had little rhymes printed on the wrappers.

The business was still holding on five years later, when Henry Hershey turned up, after a long absence, with some candy-display cases he had had made for promoting his failed cough drops. Milton bought them for $350, and Henry headed for the silver mines of Colorado. The useless cabinets seemed to weigh on Milton's spirits, and he suffered a moderate nervous breakdown, leaving the candy business to the women and one employee until he could recover. Not long after this the firm's delivery horse bolted, tipping over a wagonload of candies, which were a total loss. This finished the M. S. Hershey business in Philadelphia, and Milton, with his mother and aunt, returned to Lancaster with nothing left of the enterprise but a few candy kettles. Hershey was twenty-five years old.

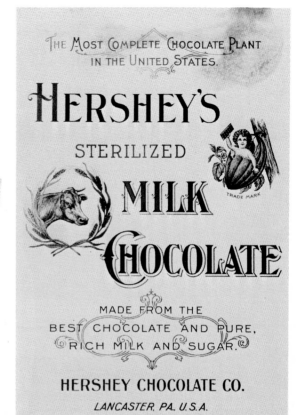

8

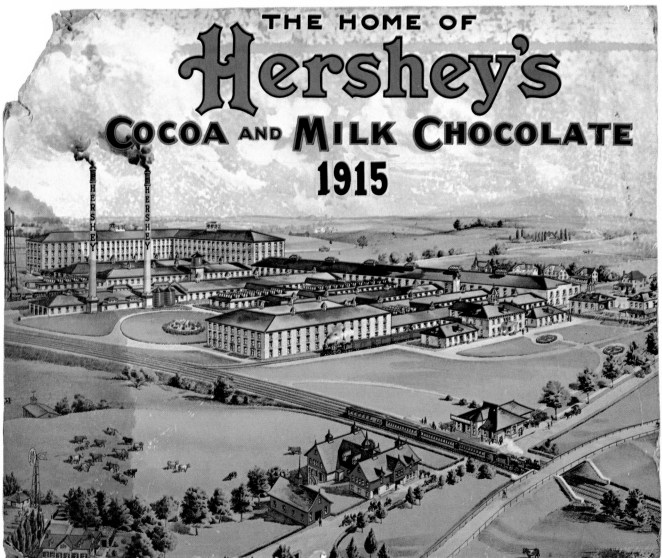

THE HOME OF
Hershey's
COCOA AND MILK CHOCOLATE
1915

Much to the dismay of advertising executives, the Hershey name became well-known to sweet-tooth Americans throughout the nation even though the company did not advertise in the media until 1970. Instead, the founder plugged his wide assortment of chocolate wares on colorful labels, tins, wrappers, and posters; perhaps his most famous promotion of all was the town that he built. It adorns the poster above, made when Hershey, Pennsylvania, was but twelve years old. The packaging above and on the opposite page harks back to the days before and after Hershey settled in Hershey and shows a certain penchant for catering to popular fancies—thus the quick-energy tablets for sports types, nourishing cocoa for the health-minded, and the patriotic chocolate cigarettes named for Dewey's flagship.

Within a few weeks optimism returned to Hershey's spirit, and he travelled to Denver to join his father. He found a job with a caramel maker there and learned the advantages in taste and quality of adding fresh milk to the candy-making process. When his father moved to Chicago to take work as a carpenter, Milton followed him, and soon the two were starting up another new candy business together—until they loaned all the firm's capital to a friend who failed to repay it. Milton tried New Orleans, and then, in 1883, he attacked New York City, working days in Huyler's candy factory and boiling his own candy at night in his landlady's kitchen. Soon he had his own candy store on Sixth Avenue, near Bryant Park. Within a few months he enthusiastically moved to larger quarters on West Forty-third Street, assuming he would be able to break the lease on the first store, but discovered he could not. The payment of double rent was about to break him, so to the rescue came his mother and Aunt Mattie—and his father as well, who set out to sell his son's wares off a pushcart. Milton was still losing money, but, like a gambler, he impetuously ordered ten thousand dollars' worth of new candy machinery on credit. Shortly after this another horse dumped another wagonload of merchandise into the street, and the New York business was finished for good. Milton had only the clothes in his rented room—until a thief stole those. So it was back to Lancaster once again.

Out on the streets with a pushcart full of homemade

CONTINUED ON PAGE 91

Right: the Hersheys with guests in a serene pose by the pool of their estate in 1909. He is at far right, she at far left. Four years later, while on a trip to Europe to consult health experts on his wife's chronic illness, Hershey took a side tour to Egypt, above. Unfortunately, the trip's purpose failed: Kitty died in 1915.

BOTH: HERSHEY FOODS CORPORATION

BEYOND MOTHER'S KNEE

EARLY AMERICAN MALE CHAUVINIST PIGS REGARDED

LITERACY FOR WOMEN WITH SCANT ENTHUSIASM.

LEARNING TO READ WAS THE FIRST FEMINIST TRIUMPH

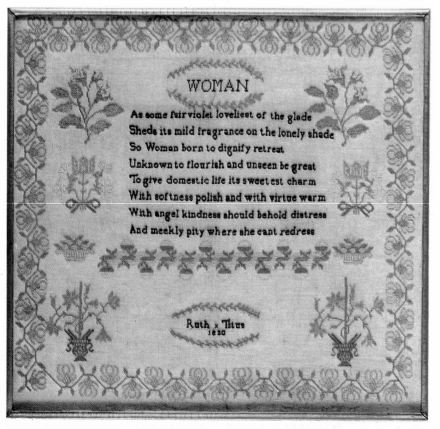

WOMAN

As some fair violet loveliest of the glade
Sheds its mild fragrance on the lonely shade
So Woman born to dignify retreat
Unknown to flourish and unseen be great
To give domestic life its sweetest charm
With softness polish and with virtue warm
With angel kindness should behold distress
And meekly pity where she cant redress

Ruth x Titus
1820

In a dainty sampler, cross-stitched on linen, goodwife Ruth Titus described the prevailing role of Woman in 1820. The operative words are "unknown," "unseen," and "meekly."

Could I have died a martyr in the cause, and thus ensured its success, I could have blessed the faggot and hugged the stake." The cause was state support for female education, the would-be Saint Joan was Emma Willard, and the rhetorical standards of the 1820's were lofty and impassioned. The most militant feminists rarely scale such heights today.

For one thing, dogged effort has finally reduced the supply of grand injustices; and today's preference for less florid metaphor has deprived the movement of such dramatic images. Comparatively speaking, the rest of the struggle is a downhill run, leading straight to twenty-four-hour day-care centers, revised and updated forms of marriage, free access to

the executive suite, and rows of "Ms's" on Senate office doors. Glorying in our headway, we easily forget that leverage comes with literacy, and literacy for women is a relative novelty.

Long before the Revolution, American males already had Harvard, Yale, and Princeton, as well as a full range of other educational institutions—grammar schools, academies, seminaries, and numerous smaller colleges. American girls had only their mother's knee. By 1818, the year in which Emma Willard first introduced her *Plan for the Improvement of Female Education,* the gap was almost as wide as ever. Public schooling was a local option, quite whimsically interpreted. The towns could provide as much or as little as they wished, extending or restricting attendance as they saw fit. Ms. Willard presented her novel proposals to the New York State legislature, which dealt with the question by putting it repeatedly at the bottom of the agenda until the session was safely over. Lavish tributes to Mother's Knee filled the halls of Albany. In the opinion of the senators, M.'s K. not only outshone our men's colleges but also Oxford, Cambridge, and Heidelberg as an institution of female edification. Despite the support of De Witt Clinton, John Adams, and Thomas Jefferson, it was three more years—when a building and grounds were offered independently by the town of Troy— before the Willard Seminary actually got under way. The academy still

By ELAINE KENDALL

flourishes and claims to "mark the beginning of higher education for women in the United States." Since that is not precisely the same as being the first such school and the rival contenders have either vanished or metamorphosed into other sorts of institutions entirely, there is no reason to dispute it. The pre-Revolutionary South did have a few early convents, including one at New Orleans that was established by the Ursuline order in 1727 and taught religion, needlework, and something of what was called basic skills. Other religious groups, particularly the Moravians and Quakers, supported female seminaries during the eighteenth century, but these places did not really attempt to offer advanced education—a commodity for which there was little market in an era when girls were unwelcome in elementary schools. A few New England clergymen opened small academies for girls during the first decade of the nineteenth century, but these noble and well-intentioned efforts were ephemeral, never outlasting their founders. Until Emma Willard succeeded in extracting that bit of real estate from Troy, public and private support for such ventures was virtually nonexistent.

Some few ambitious and determined girls did succeed in learning to read and write in colonial America, but hardly ever at public expense and certainly not in comfort. Their number was pitifully small, and those who gained more than the rudiments of literacy would hardly have crowded a saltbox parlor. The early Puritans apparently stretched Saint Paul's dogma "I permit not a woman to teach" to mean that women should not be allowed to learn, either. John Winthrop's *History of New England from 1630 to 1649* tells what happened when a group of women met for what seems to have been a discussion of great issues. The town fathers decided that "though women might meet (some few together) to pray and

edify one another; yet such a set assembly (as was then in practice at Boston) where sixty or more did meet every week, and one woman (in a prophetical way, by resolving questions of doctrine and expounding scripture) took upon her the whole exercise, was agreed to be disorderly, and without rule." Anne Hutchinson, the instigator of such a group, was banished by an inquisition that could have been conducted by Torquemada himself. She was branded a heretic and exiled to Rhode Island. Her persecutors trailed her there and eventually drove her to the hostile wilds of Long Island, where the entire Hutchinson family was murdered by Indians.

Nor was the Puritan attitude much friendlier toward women who sought only to educate themselves. As the poet Anne Bradstreet wrote bitterly during the 1650's:

For such despite they cast on female wits.
If what I do prove well, it won't advance,
They'l say its stoln, or else it was
    by chance.

As the grip of Puritanism gradually relaxed, the image of a learned female improved infinitesimally. She was no longer regarded as a disorderly person or a heretic but merely as a nuisance to her husband, family, and friends. A sensible woman soon found ways to conceal her little store of knowledge or, if hints of it should accidentally slip out, to disparage or apologize for it. Abigail Adams, whose wistful letters show a continuing interest in women's education, described her own with a demurely rhymed disclaimer:

The little learning I have gained
Is all from simple nature drained.

In fact, the wife of John Adams was entirely self-educated. She disciplined herself to plod doggedly through works of ancient history whenever her household duties permitted, being careful to do so in the

privacy of her boudoir. In her letters she deplored the fact that it was still customary to "ridicule female learning" and even in the "best families" to deny girls more than the barest rudiments.

The prevailing colonial feeling toward female education was still so unanimously negative that it was not always thought necessary to mention it. Sometimes this turned out to be a boon. A few villages, in their haste to establish schools for boys, neglected to specify that only males would be admitted. From the beginning they wrote their charters rather carelessly, using the loose generic term "children." This loophole was nearly always blocked as soon as the risks became apparent, but in the interim period of grace girls were occasionally able to pick up a few crumbs of knowledge. They did so by sitting outside the schoolhouse or on its steps, eavesdropping on the boys' recitations. More rarely, girls were tolerated in the rear of the schoolhouse behind a curtain, in a kind of makeshift seraglio. This Levantine arrangement, however, was soon abandoned as inappropriate to the time and place, and the attendance requirements were made unambiguous. New England winters and Cape Cod architecture being what they are, the amount of learning that one could have acquired by these systems was necessarily scanty. Still it was judged excessive. The female scholars in the yard and on the stairs seemed to suffer disproportionately from pleurisy and other respiratory ailments. Further proof of the divine attitude toward the educating of women was not sought. Girls were excluded for their own good, as well as to ensure the future of the Colonies.

After the Revolution the atmosphere in the New England states did become considerably more lenient. Here and there a town council might vote to allow girls inside the school building from five to seven in the morning, from six to eight at night, or, in a few very liberal communities, during the few weeks in summer when the boys were at work in the fields or shipyards. This was a giant step forward and would have been epochal if teachers had always appeared at these awkward times. Unfortunately the girls often had to muddle through on their own without benefit of faculty. The enlightened trend, moreover, was far from general. In 1792 the town of Wellesley, Massachusetts, voted "not to be at any expense for schooling girls," and similarly worded bylaws were quite usual throughout the northern states until the 1820's. In the southern Colonies, where distances between the great estates delayed the beginnings of any public schooling even longer, wealthy planters often imported tutors to instruct their sons in academic subjects. If they could afford the additional luxury, they might also engage singing and dancing masters for the daughters, who were not expected to share their brothers' more arduous lessons. In a pleasant little memoir of the South, *Colonial Days and Dames,* Anne Wharton, a descendant of Thomas Jefferson, noted that "very little from books was thought necessary for a girl. She was trained to domestic matters . . . the accomplishments of the day . . . to play upon the harpsichord or spinet, and to work impossible dragons and roses upon canvas."

Although the odds against a girl's gaining more than the sketchiest training during this era seem to have been overwhelming, there were some remarkable exceptions. The undiscouraged few included Emma Willard herself; Catherine and Harriet Beecher, the clergyman's daughters, who established an early academy at Hartford; and Mary Lyon, who founded the college that began in 1837 as Mount Holyoke Seminary. Usually, however, the tentative and halfhearted experiments permitted by the New England towns served only to give aid and comfort to the opposition. They seemed to show that the female mind was not inclined to scholarship and the female body was not strong enough to withstand ex-

Frontispiece from an 1822 girls' textbook

posure—*literal* exposure, in many cases—to it. By 1830 or so primary education had been grudgingly extended to girls almost everywhere, but it was nearly impossible to find anyone who dared champion any further risks. Boston had actually opened a girls' high school in 1826 only to abolish it two years later. The closing notice mentioned the fact that the institution had been "an alarming success." Shaken, the town fathers did not allow another trial for twenty years. New Englanders have long memories, and the legend of poor Mistress Hopkins, the wife of one of Connecticut's early colonial governors, was revived as a cautionary tale and repeated whenever the subject of female education was raised. She had, it seemed, gone mad from mental exertion. "For if she had attended her household affairs, and such things as belong to women," wrote John Winthrop, "and not gone out of her way and calling to meddle in such things as are proper for men, whose minds are stronger, etc., she had kept her wits." Widespread pity for Mistress Hopkins lasted for almost two hundred years, a powerful deterrent to progress. The unfortunate lady became a standard text for countless sermons, thus achieving a sadly ironic immortality.

Having heard less about the awful consequences of study, the Middle Atlantic Colonies seem to have been more willing to gamble, and the Dutch who settled New York tolerated girls in their primary schools from the very beginning. These were church sponsored, and strict and total segregation was the rule. Smaller towns with only one building at their disposal specified that "Boys and Girls should be separated as much as possible from each other." Girls again got the drafty back rows and the chilly corners. The good burghers of New Amsterdam took particular pains to guarantee that their thrifty mixing of the sexes did

The "new science" of calisthenics was added to the curriculum of young ladies' seminaries in the early nineteenth century. It wasn't hard for educators to prove that girls who flexed a few muscles on trapeze or horizontal bar remained healthier than their less active sisters. To no one's surprise, the gymnasts' costumes were unfailingly decorous.

not encourage social evils. School rules spelled out the punishments to be used upon those "Who chase or throw at peoples' ducks or animals; who run their hands thru their hairs; who buy candy; Who throw their bread to dogs or cats; who spit in the drink of another or step on his dinner." These offenses were impartially dealt with by whipping, though there is no certain way of knowing whether running the hands through the hairs drew as many strokes as spitting in a classmate's drink. In any case the Dutch primary schools, even when co-ed, sound rather grim. In addition to the Bible and catechisms, boys and girls alike studied *Exquisite Proofs of Man's Misery, Last Wills,* and *Hours of Death.* Many of the girl students, after this taste of equality and the joys of erudition, left school before learning to write. In fact, few of them even stayed long enough to read, and the largest percentage, perhaps discouraged by the grisly offerings, never attended at all. The curriculum seemed expressly designed to produce the highest possible dropout rate. The girls could hardly be blamed for low motivation, since they had an approved and tempting alternative. It was much easier and more pleasant to stay home and learn to cook, weave, spin, brew beer, and tend children in the cheerful company of their sisters and friends. The boys must have envied them. Despite their apparent generosity, the Dutch settlers managed to achieve an even higher rate of female illiteracy than the adamant Puritans, and they accomplished it without discriminatory laws. The courthouse files of wills, deeds, and marriages indicate 60

per cent of New York women were unable to read or write during the colonial period. In New England, despite the obstacles, approximately 60 per cent could at least sign their names.

Public schools obviously were not the only route to learning or most female American children up through colonial times would have been doomed to total ignorance. Fathers, especially clergymen fathers, would often drill their daughters in the Bible and sometimes teach them to read and do simple sums as

JOHN JENKINS, *Art of Writing,* 1813

Learning the fine art of penmanship

well. Nothing that enhanced an understanding of the Scriptures could be entirely bad, and arithmetic was considered useful in case a woman were to find herself the sole support of her children. Brothers would sometimes lend or hand down their old school books, and fond uncles might

help a favorite and clever niece with her sums. The boys' tutor was often amenable to a pretty sister's pleas for lessons. For those girls not fortunate enough to be the daughters of foresighted New England parsons or wealthy tobacco and cotton factors, most colonial towns provided dame schools. These catered to boys as well as to girls of various ages. They offered a supplement to the curriculum at Mother's Knee, but only just. Because these schools were kept by women who had acquired their own learning haphazardly, the education they offered was motley at best. The solitary teacher could impart no more than she herself knew, and that rarely exceeded the alphabet, the shorter catechism, sewing, knitting, some numbers, and perhaps a recipe for baked beans and brown bread. The actual academic function of these early American institutions seems to have been somewhat exaggerated and romanticized by historians. Dame schools were really no more than small businesses, managed by impoverished women who looked after neighborhood children and saw to it that idle little hands did not make work for the devil. The fees (tuition is too grand a word) were tiny, with threepence a week per child about par. That sum could hardly have paid for a single hornbook for the entire class. The dame school itself was an English idea, transplanted almost intact to the Colonies. Several seem to have been under way by the end of the seventeenth century. A typical example was described by George Crabbe:

When a deaf poor patient widow sits
And awes some twenty infants as she knits

Infants of humble, busy wives who pay
Some trifling price for freedom through
the day
. . . .
Her room is small, they cannot widely
stray
Her threshold high, they cannot run
away. . . .

As early as 1682 the town of Springfield, Massachusetts, permitted Goodwife Mirick to establish one of these prototypical day-care centers, and the dame schools continued as the main fount of female education for more than a hundred years. We can be reasonably sure that they didn't violate the prevailing notions about female teaching and learning. Crabbe's poem was written in the 1780's, and there had been few changes in the intervening century. With rare good luck a child might get a competent schoolmistress like Miriam Wood of Dorchester, whose epitaph notes that "when she died, she scarcely left her mate"—mate, in this case, meaning peer, not husband—but quite often the dame seems to have been less than ideally qualified for her job. There were not many like Miriam Wood, and the New England court records are enlivened by reprimands to these women for their shortcomings. Some dozed through the day, others tippled, and there is one instance of a New Haven dame charged with "Prophane Swearing." (It is recorded that her profanity was "By my soul!") In this last unhappy case it was a small female pupil who was hauled into court, despite her plea that she had learned the offending phrase from her teacher.

As the country became more affluent, schoolkeeping gradually began to attract more ambitious types. Older girls were still being excluded from the town seminaries and in many places from the grammar schools as well. A great many people quickly realized that there was money to be made by teaching the children of the new middle class and

that they could sell their services for far more than pennies. No special accreditation or qualification was required, and there was no competition from the state. Toward the end of the eighteenth century and at the beginning of the nineteenth, platoons of self-styled professors invaded American towns and cities, promising to instruct both sexes and all ages in every known art, science, air, and grace. These projects were popularly known as adventure schools, a phrase that has a pleasant modern ring to it, suggesting open classrooms, free electives, and individual attention.

That, however, is deceptive. The people who ran such schools were usually adventurers in the not very admirable sense of the word: unscrupulous, self-serving, and of doubtful origins and attainments. Many simply equipped themselves with false diplomas and titles from foreign universities and set up shop. The schools continued to operate only as long as they turned a profit. When enrollment dropped, interest waned, or fraud became obvious, the establishment would simply fold and the proprietors move to another town for a fresh start. The newer territories were particularly alluring to the worst of these entrepreneurs, since their reputations could neither precede nor follow them there. A new name, a new prospectus, an ad in the gazette, and they were in business again until scandal or mismanagement obliged them to move on. Such "schools" were not devised for the particular benefit of girls; but because they were independent commercial enterprises, no solvent person was turned away. Thousands of young women did take advantage of the new opportunity and were, in many cases, taken advantage of in return. For boys the adventure schools were an alternative to the strict classicism and religiosity of the academies and seminaries, but for girls they were the only educational pos-

sibility between the dame school and marriage.

There was little effort to devise a planned or coherent course of study, though elaborately decorated certificates were awarded upon completion of a series of lessons. The scholar could buy whatever he or she fancied from a mind-bending list. One could take needlework at one place, languages at another, dancing or "ouranology" at a third. (It was a pompous era, and no one was fonder of polysyllables than the professors. Ouranology was sky-watching, but it sounded impressive.) There were no minimum or maximum course requirements, though the schoolmasters naturally made every effort to stock the same subjects offered by the competition, in order to reduce the incidence of school-hopping. By the end of the eighteenth century, according to a nineteenth-century educator, a prosperous New Yorker had a choice of "reading, writing, and arithmetic; Low Dutch, English, French, Latin, Greek; merchants' accounts, algebra, logarithmetical and instrumental arithmetic, geometry, trigonometry, plain [*sic*] or spherical, surveying, gauging, dialling, mensuration of superficies and solids; astronomy, the calculation of and projection of the eclipses of the luminaries, planets, places, the projection of the sphere upon the plan of any circle; navigation, uses of charts and globes, geography, anatomy and midwifery." That list is only partial, but it is representative of the higher studies for sale during the Revolutionary era. The catalogues were protean, but it is impossible to discover how many of these courses were ever available at any given time. The masters of such schools must certainly have left themselves some outs comparable to those in contemporary college bulletins—"not given in the winter of 1779-80," "offered only to groups of ten or more," "may be elected only by those who have fulfilled the prerequisites." There was

CONTINUED ON PAGE 73

Guilford Court House

A private of the Delaware Regiment   A private of the 71st Regiment of Foot

Major General Nathanael Greene, commanding the Continental Army in the south, spent mid-March of 1781 trying to lure Cornwallis and his army into battle on advantageous ground. He had to do it quickly, for the enlistments of many of his soldiers would soon expire. Greene finally deployed his troops on the high ground surrounding Guilford Court House in North Carolina. Cornwallis took the bait and began to move against him with some two thousand men. Although Greene had more than twice that number, most of them were shaky militia whose reaction to battle was wholly unpredictable. Greene planned accordingly. He posted untried North Carolinians across the probable path of the enemy and, grinning encouragement, told them to fire only two volleys before they ran away. Behind these men was a tougher line of Virginians, and behind them the rock of Greene's makeshift army, indestructible Maryland and Delaware regiments. The units took up their final positions on the cool, bright morning of March 15.

The first blood of the day was spilled in a sharp cavalry brush when Colonel Henry "Light-Horse Harry" Lee's men cut up a column of Colonel Banastre Tarleton's hated dragoons and retired toward the main body of the Continental Army with the British advance close on their heels.

The English and Hessian troops came out of the woods in formal line of battle, and the Carolinians fired their two volleys and fled. The British pressed forward behind level bayonets, but steady American riflemen knocked large gaps in their ranks. The attack faltered and stopped as American units backed up by Colonel William Washington's cavalrymen plunged in among the British files. For a few bloody minutes it looked as though the Continentals were going to win the field. Then Cornwallis, in a desperate decision, turned his artillery on the chaos, spraying his own soldiers as well as the Americans with grape. Gradually the two armies separated and drew apart. The exhausted Continentals waited for the fighting to resume, but Greene, realizing that he had hurt the British badly and loath to gamble the only American army in the south, wisely ordered a retreat.

The Americans pulled back through a dismal, chilly rain. They had suffered a long and grueling day and, strictly speaking, a defeat. But they were by no means disheartened. British losses had been twice theirs, and the weary men knew they were leaving a shaken enemy behind them. And though none of them could know it at the time, they were close now to a victory worth a hundred Guilfords; soon Cornwallis would begin his long retreat that would end, a half year later, at Yorktown. —R.F.S.

Third in a series of paintings for

A Continental field officer, hat in hand, exhorts soldiers of the 1st Maryland Regiment to attack the British in the climactic moments of the Battle of Guilford Court House. Standing against them are troopers of the combined brigade of Guards and grenadiers, already re-forming their ranks, which were scattered by a charge of Colonel William Washington's dragoons. A few dragoons are still visible to the right of the picture,

sickling the English infantrymen with their long cavalry sabers. In the distance the 71st Regiment of Foot is seen dimly through the smoke, marching forward to support their beleaguered countrymen. The surprisingly well-clad Marylanders in the foreground had been issued new uniforms not long before. Their muskets had either been begged from the French or taken from British and Hessian soldiers in earlier battles.

"In such moments all fears of death are over"

Major General Nathanael Greene, Continental Army:

. . . I took the resolution of attacking the enemy without loss of time, and made the necessary disposition accordingly, being persuaded, that if we were successful, it would prove ruinous to the enemy, and, if otherwise, it would only prove a partial evil to us.

The army marched from the High-rock ford on the 12th, and on the 14th arrived at Guildford. . . .

Lieutenant Colonel Henry Lee, Continental Army:

The country to a wide extent around, waste and rolling, was covered with lofty trees and thick shrubby underwood. Narrow tangled glades wound between the hills and . . . dripped their scant rills into a larger stream . . . that crossed the great Salisbury road, about two miles from the courthouse. The melancholy horror, the wild sterility, and the lonely aspect of the scene, seemed ready to overawe the rage, and to welcome the fears of men.

Major General Nathanael Greene, Continental Army:

. . . On the morning of the 15th, our reconnoitering party reported the enemy advancing on the great Salisbury road. . . .

. . . Lieutenant-colonel [Henry] Lee . . . met the enemy on their advance, and had a severe skirmish with Lieutenant-colonel [Banastre] Tarleton, in which the enemy suffered greatly. . . .

The action commenced by a cannonade, which lasted about twenty minutes, when the enemy advanced in three columns; the Hessians on the right, the guards in the center, and Lieutenant-colonel [James] Webster's brigade on the left. The whole moved through the old fields to attack the North-Carolina brigades. . . .

Sergeant Roger Lamb, British Army:

. . . After the brigade formed across the open ground, the colonel [Webster] rode on to the front, and gave the word, *"Charge."* Instantly the movement was made, in excellent order, in a smart run, with arms charged: when arrived within forty yards of the enemy's line, it was perceived that their whole force had their arms presented, and resting on a rail fence, the common partitions in America. They were taking aim with the nicest precision. . . . At this awful period a general pause took place; both parties surveyed each other for the moment with the most anxious suspense. . . . [Then] colonel Webster rode forward in the front of the 23d regiment, and said, with more than even his usual commanding voice . . . *"Come on, my brave Fuzileers."* This operated like an inspiring voice, they rushed forward amidst the enemy's fire; dreadful was the havoc on both sides. . . . At last the Americans gave way,

and the brigade advanced, to the attack of their second line. Here the conflict became still more fierce. Before it was completely routed, where I stood . . . I observed an American officer attempting to fly. I immediately darted after him, but he perceiving my intention to capture him, fled with the utmost speed. I pursued, and was gaining on him, when, hearing a confused noise on my left, I observed several bodies of Americans drawn up within the distance of a few yards. Whoever has been in an engagement well knows that, in such moments all fears of death are over. . . . I had no time for deliberation. How to act I knew not. On the instant, however, I saw lord Cornwallis riding across the clear ground. His lordship was mounted on a dragoon's horse (his own having been shot;) . . . his lordship was evidently unconscious of his danger. I immediately laid hold of the bridle of his horse, and . . . mentioned to him, that if his lordship had pursued the same direction, he would in a few moments have been surrounded by the enemy. . . . I continued to run along side of the horse, keeping the bridle in my hand, until his lordship gained the 23d regiment. . . .

Lieutenant Colonel Henry Lee, Continental Army:

. . . The throes and gestures of this strife . . . it is impossible to describe; the deadly and determined thrusts of the infantry, the rush and spurning of the chargers, and the murderous slashing of the fierce dragoons. . . . The guards fell in heaps around the guns they had taken; and their leader slain, were driven back into the open ground; many prostrated by the horse—many killed or captured by the pursuing infantry. The remnant fled for protection to their friends, but received the balls directed at their enemies; for Cornwallis, with furious decision, ordered his artillery to fire, sacrificing the fugitives to check the pursuit. . . .

Lieutenant Colonel Banastre Tarleton, British Army:

At this period the event of the action was doubtful, and victory alternately presided over each army. . . . At this crisis, the judicious use of the three pounders, the firm countenance of the British infantry, and the appearance of the cavalry, obliged the enemy to retreat. . . .

Lieutenant Colonel Henry Lee, Continental Army:

In this battle, the victory of the British general was complete, but to himself disastrous; his glory was great, but his loss prodigious. Nearly one third of his troops were killed or wounded, while the loss of the Americans did not exceed one twelfth—facts which, as soon as they were ascertained, gave predominance to the republicans in North Carolina, and made Greene a conqueror, and Cornwallis a fugitive.

WHAT POLIOMYELITIS MEANT
TO A POLITICAL CAREER

F.D.R's Extra Burden

By BERNARD ASBELL

This article is an excerpt from a new book on Franklin Delano Roosevelt recently published by Doubleday & Company. It is being publicized as The F.D.R. Memoirs *"as written by Bernard Asbell." Mr. Asbell undertakes to recount the story of the Roosevelt administration in the first person, as he thinks F.D.R. himself might have written it had he lived to do so. This literary ploy is sure to excite controversy, and one might reasonably fear that in years to come, confused or careless readers will attribute to Franklin D. Roosevelt observations actually made by Bernard Asbell. However, Mr. Asbell has anchored each of his plausible but fictive chapters with a "background memorandum," using more conventional historical methods and showing the private experiences in F.D.R.'s life that were especially relevant to the foregoing chapter. Roosevelt is a familiar field for him, since he was the author of the best-selling* When F.D.R. Died *(1961). The following excerpt is adapted from the "background memorandum" for a chapter dealing with F.D.R.'s campaign of 1936.*

Every campaigner, especially for leadership of a large and complex state or for national office, is a cripple.

His legs are bound against running faster than his constituents are able to keep in step. His hands are tied by the limited powers of the office he seeks; he had better not promise what he knows he cannot deliver. His tongue is gagged against pronouncements that may make new friends if those pronouncements will also make new enemies. His balance is threatened by the pulls and tugs of conflicting demands for justice—shall money go for this urgent need or that one?—shall this group's freedom be expanded at the expense of that one's?

Immobilized by these paralyzing constraints, the candidate has to make himself appear able-bodied, attractive, confident, and powerful. At least more so than his opponent.

Being crippled—not in metaphor, but in reality—is perhaps good schooling for politics.

To this day, more than a quarter

century after his death, people keep wondering aloud and speculating, "If Roosevelt had not been a cripple, would he have been the same kind of President?" Of course not. "If a different kind, how?" Impossible to say. "If he had not been a cripple, would he have become President at all?" Again, imponderable.

Did F.D.R.'s private battle teach him to identify with those who suffer? Unquestionably. Moreover it taught him the uses of patience (never a strong suit with crusaders who relied upon him, upon whom he relied, yet who continually harassed him). It heightened his sense of time and timing. "It made him realize"—an observation of Egbert Curtis, a Warm Springs companion—"that he was not infallible, that everything wasn't always going to go his way." More than anything, it forced him to study the uses of handicap, paradoxically giving him a leg up in a profession of able-bodied crippled men.

Let's not carry theory and speculation too far. Instead, let's try to observe firsthand, insofar as the written word permits, the connections between suffering and Roosevelt's acquired capacity for patience, for tolerance and respect of the wills and ambitions of others, for turning handicap into power.

We begin with his own words. A sufferer identifies with sufferers; and "Doctor" Roosevelt of Warm Springs also identified with other doctors. In F.D.R.'s early days at Warm Springs a South Carolina physician wrote to Roosevelt for a personal case report that might help him treat any polio patient who came his way. Roosevelt's reply is the only detailed personal account of what he had recently endured. The letter, dictated to Missy LeHand, his private secretary, during their first stay at Warm Springs, says in part:

... I am very glad to tell you what I can in regard to my case and as I have talked it over with a great many doctors can, I think, give you a history of the case which would be equal to theirs.

First symptoms of the illness appeared in August, 1921. . . . By the end of the third day practically all muscles from the chest down were involved. Above the chest the only symptom was a weakening of the two large thumb muscles making it impossible to write. There was no special pain along the spine and no rigidity of the neck.

For the following two weeks I had to be catheterized and there was slight, though not severe, difficulty in controlling the bowels. The fever lasted for only 6 or 7 days, but all the muscles from the hips down were extremely sensitive to the touch and I had to have the knees supported by pillows. This condition of extreme discomfort lasted about 3 weeks . . . [but] disappeared gradually over a period of six months, the last remaining point being the calf muscles.

As to treatment—the mistake was made for the first 10 days of giving my feet and lower legs rather heavy massage. This was stopped by Dr. Lovett, of Boston, who was, without doubt, the greatest specialist on infantile paralysis. In January, 1922, 5 months after the attack, he found that the muscles behind the knees had contracted and that there was a tendency to footdrop in the right foot. These were corrected by the use of plaster casts during two weeks. In February, 1922, braces were fitted on each leg from the hips to the shoes, and I was able to stand up and learned gradually to walk with crutches. At the same time gentle exercises were begun, first every other day, then daily, exercising each muscle 10 times and seeking to avoid any undue strain by giving each muscle the correct movement with gravity. These exercises I did on a board placed on the bed.

The recovery of muscle paralysis began at this time, though for many months it seemed to make little progress. In the summer of 1922 I began swimming and found that this exercise seemed better adapted than any other because all weight was removed from the legs and I was able to move the legs in the water far better than I had expected. . . .

I still wear braces, of course, because the quadriceps are not yet strong enough to bear my weight. One year ago I was able to stand in fresh water without braces when the water was up to my chin. Six months ago I could stand in water up to the top of my shoulders and today can stand in water just level with my arm pits. This is a very simple method for me of determining how fast the quadriceps are coming back. Aside from these muscles the waist muscles on the right side are still weak and the outside muscles on the right leg have strengthened so much more than the inside muscles that they pull my right foot forward. I continue corrective exercises for all the muscles.

To sum up I would give you the following "Don'ts":

Don't use heavy massage but use light massage rubbing always towards the heart.

Don't let the patient over-exercise any muscle or get tired.

Don't let the patient feel cold, especially the legs, feet or any other part affected. Progress stops entirely when the legs or feet are cold.

Don't let the patient get too fat.

The following treatment is so far the best, judging from my own experience and that of hundreds of other cases which I have studied:

1. Gentle exercise especially for the muscles which seem to be worst affected.

2. Gentle skin rubbing—not muscle kneading—bearing in mind that good circulation is a prime requisite.

3. Swimming in warm water—lots of it.

4. Sunlight—all the patient can get, especially direct sunlight on the affected parts. It would be ideal to lie in the sun all day with nothing on. This is difficult to accomplish but the nearest approach to it is a bathing suit.

5. Belief on the patient's part that the muscles are coming back and will eventually regain recovery of the affected parts. There are cases known in Norway where adults have taken the disease and not been able to walk until after a lapse of 10 or even 12 years.

I hope that your patient has not got a very severe case. They all differ, of course, in the degree in which the parts are affected. If braces are necessary there is a man in New York . . . who makes remarkable light braces of duraluminum. My first braces of steel weighed 7 lbs. apiece—my new ones weigh only 4 lbs. apiece. Remember that braces are only for the convenience of the patient in getting around—a leg in a brace does not have a chance for muscle development. This muscle development must come through exercise when the brace is not on—such as swimming, etc.

At Hyde Park, before discovering Warm Springs, this powerful man, to the shock of his children and friends, practiced dragging himself crablike

HARRIS & EWING
—PHOTO TRENDS

Left: Just a year before polio struck at Campobello, an ebullient F.D.R. campaigned for the Vice-Presidency in the summer of 1920. Opposite: Some eight years later he posed in a carefully practiced stance, supported by a heavy cane and the rigid arm of his son Elliott.

across the floor, explaining that the one fear he ever knew was that of being caught in a fire. Then, showing off his inordinately strong shoulders and arms, he filled the house with laughter, wrestling his boys on the floor two at a time. His mother ordered an electric tricycle from Europe, but F.D.R. used it only once. He didn't want his muscles *worked*; he wanted to work them himself.

John Gunther describes Roosevelt's determination to get from floor to floor unaided: "Day after day he would haul his dead weight up the stairs by the power of his hands and arms, step by step, slowly, doggedly; the sweat would pour off his face, and he would tremble with exhaustion. Moreover he insisted on doing this with members of the family or friends watching him, and he would talk all the time as he inched himself up little by little, talk, talk, and make people talk back. It was a kind of enormous spiritual catharsis—as if he had to do it, to prove his independence, and had to have the feat witnessed, to prove that it was nothing."

At Warm Springs in 1924 he concentrated on the day he would be able to walk unaided with braces. Braces, which he once said he "hated and mistrusted," which he could not put on or take off by himself, made him like a man on stilts. Unable to flex his toes, he had no balance. In 1928, after seven years of immobility and more than four years of daring and persevering, one day, finally, triumphantly, he hobbled most of the way across the living-room floor of his cottage— with braces, but without human help. The achievement was exhausting— and was never to be accomplished again. Years later, according to Grace Tully, "Missy's eyes filled up when on occasions she reminisced about those days." Roosevelt liked to maintain the belief that if he had had another year before the demand that he run for governor, he'd have mastered walking with a single brace.

In the summer of 1928 at Warm

Springs, shortly after Roosevelt agreed to address the Democratic National Convention at Houston, son Elliott, eighteen, was visiting. One evening Roosevelt was lost in concentrated thought when suddenly he burst out:

"With my hand on a man's arm, *and one cane*—I'm sure. Let's try it!"

A fellow polio victim, Turnley Walker, Roosevelt's dinner guest, described what then happened and was repeated over and over:

First Roosevelt would get over to the wall and balance there with his cane. It was an ordinary cane but he held it in a special way, with his index finger extended down along the rod from the handle. This finger acted as a rigid cleat . . . so that the strength of the massive arm and shoulder rammed straight along the cane to its tip against the floor.

"Now, Elliott, you get on the left, my weak side." Elliott watchfully took his place and [Helena] Mahoney [a physiotherapist] came forward to show him how to hold his right arm against his middle at the proper angle and lock it there with a clenching of his biceps.

"Remember that a polio needs more than a fingertip of guidance—he needs an *iron bar*," said Mahoney. "Make a habit of *holding that arm there*. Never forget the job it's got to do."

"Let's go," said Roosevelt, and he reached out to find the proper grip. Elliott had never felt his father's hand touching him that way. He had been grabbed and hugged, and even tossed and caught with wild energy when he was younger. But now the fingers sought their grip with a kind of ruthless desperation. . . . The pressure became stronger than he had expected as his father pressed down to hitch one braced leg forward for the first step. "You must *go right with him*," said

WIDE WORLD

23

Mahoney sternly. "Watch his feet. Match your strides with his." Elliott stared down as the rigid feet swung out slowly, and through the pressing hand he could feel the slow, clenching effort of his father's powerful body.

"Don't look at me, Son. Keep your head up, smiling, watching the eyes of people. Keep them from noticing what we're doing."

The cane went out, the good leg swung, the pressure came, the weak leg hitched up into its arc and then fell stiffly into the proper place against the floor. Elliott carefully coordinated his own legs, and they moved across the room.

Roosevelt set his hips against the far wall and told Elliott to rest his arm. "We'll do beautifully," he said.

They went across the room and back again. It was becoming somewhat easier.

"As soon as you feel confident, Son, look up and around at people, the way you would do if I weren't crippled."

"But don't forget," Mahoney warned, "if he loses his balance, he'll crash down like a tree."

"Don't scare us," said Roosevelt.

. . . The cane, the swing, the pressure, the swing. Elliott found that he could look up now and then as they advanced. He caught his father's eyes, the broad smile which was held with a very slight rigidity. . . . Only then did he notice that his father was perspiring heavily.

Yet except when a public show required such extraordinary exertion, Roosevelt was as helpless as a baby. When no strangers were around to see, he let himself be carried by practiced attendants. When F.D.R. became governor, his cousin Nicholas Roosevelt spent a weekend at Hyde Park and later recalled: "His mother and I stood on the veranda watching his son Elliott and Gus Gennerich, the state trooper who acted as his personal bodyguard, carry him down the steps and place him in the car. As they turned and left him, he lost his balance (his powerful torso was much heavier than his crippled legs), and he fell over on the car seat. I doubt if one man in a thousand as disabled and dependent on others would have refrained from some sort of reproach,

however mild, to those whose carelessness had thus left him in the lurch. But Franklin merely lay on his back, waved his strong arms in the air and laughed. At once they came back and helped him to his seat behind the wheel, and he called me to join him."

Louis Howe, F.D.R.'s indispensable factotum, set an iron rule—one that F.D.R. was not inclined to resist —that he never be carried in public.

Frances Perkins remembered the gubernatorial campaign:

I saw him speak in a small hall in New York City's Yorkville district. The auditorium was crowded. . . . The only possible way for any candidate to enter the stage without being crushed by the throng was by the fire escape. I realized with sudden horror that the only way he could get over that fire escape was in the arms of strong men. That was how he arrived.

Those of us who saw this incident, with our hands on our throats to hold down our emotion, realized that this man had accepted the ultimate humility which comes from being helped physically. . . . He got up on his braces, adjusted them, straightened himself, smoothed his hair, linked his arm in his son Jim's, and walked out on the platform as if this were nothing unusual. . . . I began to see what the great teachers of religion meant when they said that humility is the greatest of virtues, and that if you can't learn it, God will teach it to you by humiliation.

Was humility—or humiliation— Roosevelt's great teacher? Many have speculated. Harold Ickes, after a day in a campaign car with press secretary Steve Early:

"[Early] recalled the campaign trips that he had made with Roosevelt when the latter was a candidate for Vice President in 1920. He said that if it hadn't been for the President's affliction, he never would have been President of the United States. In those earlier years, as Steve put it, the President was just a playboy. . . . He couldn't be made to prepare his speeches in advance, preferring to

play cards instead. During his long illness, according to Steve, the President began to read deeply and study public questions."

Perkins: ". . . He had become conscious of other people, of weak people, of human frailty. I remember thinking that he would never be so hard and harsh in judgment on stupid people—even on wrongdoers. . . . I remember watching him [as governor] in Utica. . . . Certainly some of the Democratic rank-and-file were pretty tiresome, with a lot of things to say that were of no consequence. However, he sat and nodded and smiled and said, 'That's fine,' when they reported some slight progress. I remembered, in contrast, how he had walked away from bores a few years earlier when he was in the State Senate.

"Now he could not walk away when he was bored. He listened, and out of it learned . . . that 'everybody wants to have the sense of belonging, of being on the inside,' that 'no one wants to be left out,' as he put it years later in a Columbus, Ohio, speech. . . ."

A considerably more speculative observation by Noel F. Busch, childhood neighbor of the Oyster Bay Roosevelts who grew up to be a *Time* correspondent and avid F.D.R.-watcher: "Loss of the use of one's legs has several effects on the human psyche. One is that, when deprived of the power to move around, the mind demands a substitute or compensation for this power, such as the ability to command other people to move around. That is why almost all invalids tend to be peckish and demanding. However . . . Roosevelt sublimated and refined the pardonable peevishness of the normal invalid into an administrative urge which would have had profound consequences for him even if he had never become President."

Biographer Emil Ludwig: "The privilege of remaining seated, which everyone concedes him because of his affliction, starts him off with an advantage in his intercourse with others, in the same way as the smallness of Napoleon's stature compelled everyone standing before him to bend his back a little. Certainly giants like Bismarck or Lincoln had an advantage when they appeared before men, but the same effect can be produced by the opposite, by a weakness, and as Roosevelt looks up at everyone standing in front of him, he has accustomed himself to an upward and therefore very energetic gesture of the chin which counteracts the danger of his conciliatory smile."

While never mentioning his paralysis in public (until his last speech to Congress in 1945) and seldom privately, F.D.R. could come down fiercely on those he felt mentioned it unfairly. Huey Long's tapping a straw hat on the useless Presidential knee he could take as bad manners—the other fellow's problem, not his. But when Fulton Oursler brought him a manuscript of a profile of F.D.R. by Jay Franklin to be published in *Liberty*—the editor courteously seeking F.D.R.'s reaction—Oursler saw "a red flush rise on his neck like the temperature in a thermometer." Assuming that Roosevelt was angered over some political needling, he learned otherwise:

"Mr. Oursler, there is only one statement in this article that I want corrected. The author says in this line here that I have 'never entirely recovered from infantile paralysis.' *Never recovered what?* I have never recovered the complete use of my knees. Will you *fix* that?"

His reticence to mention it—and the released heat that accompanied exceptions—were shared by Mrs. Roosevelt. At an Akron, Ohio, lecture she was asked: "Do you think your husband's illness has affected his mentality?" Betraying no emotion as she read the written question aloud, she paused for an extra cooling moment and replied: "I am glad that

question was asked. The answer is Yes. Anyone who has gone through great suffering is bound to have a greater sympathy and understanding of the problems of mankind." The audience rose in an ovation.

He was frequently torn between keeping his silence and protesting his case. On April 6, 1938, he wrote to an "old friend"—Elliott's description—mentioning his affliction. The important thing is not what he wrote but his decision not to mail it. Instead, he marked it "Written for the Record" and filed it away. It said in part:

. . . I do not mind telling you, in complete 100% confidence, that in 1923, when I first went to Florida . . . my old running mate, Jim Cox, came to see me on my house-boat in Miami. At that time I was, of course, walking with great difficulty—braces and crutches. Jim's eyes filled with tears when he saw me, and I gathered from his conversation that he was dead certain that I had had a stroke and that another one would soon completely remove me. At that time, of course, my general health was extremely good. . . .

Jim Cox from that day on always shook his head when my name was mentioned and said in sorrow that in effect I was a hopeless invalid and could never resume any active participation in business or political affairs.

As late as 1931—I think it was—when I was coming back from the Governors' Conference in Indiana, I stopped off at Dayton to see Jim Cox. He had had a very serious operation, followed by a thrombosis in his leg, and was very definitely invalided. His whole attitude during the two hours I spent with him alone was the same—that it was marvelous that I could stand the strain of the Governorship, but that in all probability I would be dead in a few months. He spent the greater part of the time asking me solicitously how I was, though he was a much sicker man than I was.

He made a fine come-back and is furious today if anybody ever refers to the thrombosis he had in his leg—but I still think he expects me to pop off at any moment.

While deciding not to mail that letter, at other times he could be as open

as a billboard. Son Jimmy recalls that on one of Madame Chiang Kai-shek's visits to the White House the grande dame thoughtlessly told the President not to stand up as she rose to leave the room. He gently replied, "My dear child, I couldn't stand up if I had to."

In a wheelchair or an automobile, getting F.D.R. into or out of an overcoat was an awkward exercise. With a stage sense of costume, F.D.R. took to a velvet-collared, braid-looped regulation Navy cape that, along with his cigarette holder, became a personal mark. Again, disadvantage was the fabric from which, with flair and style, he fashioned advantage.

Out of deference to his office as well as personal affection, newsmen virtually never mentioned the President's disability. So effective was their conspiracy, even upon themselves, that, as John Gunther recalled, "hardboiled newspaper men who knew that he could not walk as well as they knew their own names could never quite get over being startled when F.D.R. was suddenly brought into a room. The shock was greater when he wheeled himself and, of course, was greatest when he was carried; he seemed, for one thing, very small. . . . During the 1930's when I lived in Europe I repeatedly met men in important positions of state who had no idea that the President was disabled."

The people of the United States —his constituents, those from whom he drew strength and, more importantly, those who drew strength from him—knew, yet didn't know. They, too, waiting at tiny railroad depots, straining to see through the autumn sunshine the commanding figure of their President, froze at the sight of the painfully slow-motion, brace-supported step-pause-step across what seemed a torturous mile of observation platform from the train's rear door to the microphone.

It was an unexpected, unforgettable drama of frailty and strength. ☆

Men of the Revolution

-IX-

In the early summer of 1775, when the time came to appoint major generals to serve with George Washington in the Continental Army, Congress voted unanimously that Israel Putnam was to be one of them. Then in his fifty-eighth year and known universally as Old Put, he was five feet six inches tall, powerfully built, and had the face of a cherubic bulldog mounted on a jaw cut like a block of wood. More to the point, he was regarded not simply as a good soldier but as a great one; a reputation won during years of frontier warfare had hung a great fog of legends about him.

Then, as now, it was virtually impossible to distinguish fact from fiction about Putnam, but to cite a few of the exploits credited to him suggests the superman his contemporaries thought him to be. Born near Salem, Massachusetts, in 1718, he had moved in 1739 with his bride to Pomfret, Connecticut, where he purchased a farm and where, three winters later, the saga began. As retailed in awe by an early biographer, the first heroics concerned a ferocious she-wolf that had dispatched seventy of Putnam's sheep and goats in a nighttime raid. Putnam and a group of neighbors tracked the "pernicious animal" (easily, it appears, since she had lost the toes of one foot in a trap) and drove her into a cave. A series of attempts failed to smoke out the wolf before Put, disregarding the pleas of his companions, fashioned a torch from birch bark, tied a rope around his waist, and was lowered into "the deep and darksome cave." Crawling about forty feet down a narrow passage, he spotted the "glaring eye-balls" of the beast, heard the gnashing of teeth and a sullen growl as the wolf prepared to spring, and in the nick of time shot her dead and dragged her out by the ears.

He prospered as a farmer, sired ten children, and in 1755—the year of Braddock's defeat—he joined Major Robert Rogers in skirmishes around the French citadel at Crown Point. For ten years, off and on, he skirted violent death, each time escaping by a hairsbreadth. At Fort Edward in '56 fire broke out near an ammunition magazine, and Putnam (single-handed, it seems) stood between the wall of a falling building and the magazine, pouring water on the blaze, saving the garrison at the penultimate moment and emerging with hands and face dreadfully burned and his entire body blistered.

Near Fort Miller he was alone in a bateau when surprised by Indians and immediately shot the "foaming rapids" of the Hudson to elude them—a feat, his biographer said, that not only astonished the savages but convinced them that Putnam was so favored by the Great Spirit that "it would be an affront to Manitou to attempt to kill him with powder and ball." Which, presumably, is why they next tried to do away with him by burning at the stake. It was in 1758 in a skirmish near Fort Anne when Putnam was tomahawked and captured, stripped, and tied to a tree to be incinerated. Transported by the "hellish scene," Old Put's biographer described the Indians circling round the prisoner, screaming and howling deliriously as "the crackling flame began to curl around the fagots," and then suggested his hero's mental state. Perceiving that his hour was at hand, Putnam "composed his mind to bid an eternal farewell to all he held most dear" and fixed his thoughts on "a happier state of existence." Then, at the very instant when "nature was quitting its last hold on sublunary things," a French officer dashed up, scattered the burning brands, and untied his bonds.

There was a long captivity in Montreal before he was exchanged, followed by frontier service with Lord Jeffery Amherst in '60 and duty in another theatre in '62, when he accompanied a British expedition to Cuba against the Spaniards, was shipwrecked, and miraculously survived. Two years later he marched with Colonel John Bradstreet to Detroit in Pontiac's War and subsequently journeyed up the Mississippi River to see what potential existed for land speculation in those parts.

All in all, it had been quite an eventful career for a simple Connecticut farmer, but more was yet to come. The image was not diminished when colonists learned that Old Put had driven a herd of sheep from Pomfret to Boston after the British closed that port in 1774. Nor did his reputation suffer when it was told how he responded to the news of Lexington a year later: he was plowing at the time and, the story went, left the plow in the furrow, unhitched his team, and without so much as a pause to change clothes rode off toward the scene of action after sending word for his regiment to follow posthaste. In June of 1775, when the Massachusetts Committee of Safety determined to fortify Bunker Hill, opposite Boston, many colonists supposed that it was Putnam—pugnacious as ever—who was behind the decision to erect a redoubt on Breed's Hill instead, since that was a more exposed position and was almost certain to provoke an attack by the redcoats. And to Putnam, since the remark was so completely in character, went the credit for that time-honored admonition, uttered just before the battle began, "Don't fire until you see the whites of their eyes!"

The trouble with living legends, however, is that they sometimes prove less effective than they are cracked up to be—an unhappy discovery made by General George Washington during the defeat of his army on Long Island, where Putnam's ignorance of the terrain and ineptness contributed their share to the disaster. There was no doubting Israel Putnam's courage or energy or his popularity with the men in the ranks; the difficulty was that the man was a major general and as such should know about the care and conduct of an army, about logistics and topography and strategy and the movement of large bodies of troops. He ought, in short, to possess considerable intelligence and resourcefulness and be something more than a bold captain in battle. There is reason to suppose that many Continental soldiers would have followed Old Put wherever he chose to lead them, but unfortunately the qualities that had made him a renowned frontier fighter and roughhewn folk hero were not necessarily the stuff of which general officers are made, and Washington was increasingly aware of his deficiencies as time wore on. In fairness, part of the trouble may have been that Old Put was over the hill; at fifty-eight he was an elderly man as age was reckoned in that day. In any case, the long and short of it was that he was put out to pasture after 1776, never to hold an important field command.

He was placed in charge of the defenses of the Hudson Highlands in 1777 and had the misfortune to let the British capture Forts Clinton and Montgomery and burn the town of Kingston, which were all in his sector. For this lapse he was relieved of command. It was alleged at the time that torpor or ignorance or incompetence—possibly all three—were involved, but a court of inquiry cleared him of negligence or malfeasance. Probably it was a blessing that a paralytic stroke forced him into retirement late in 1779; until then the spirit remained willing and the old war-horse was still eager for battle, and there was something pathetic about the inactivity to which he had been relegated.

Back on the farm at last, he lingered on until 1790 in a manner described in the rolling hyperbole of a former companion in arms: "In patient, yet fearless expectation of the approach of THE KING OF TERRORS, whom he hath full often faced in the field of blood, the christian hero now enjoys in domestic retirement the fruit of his early industry." —*Richard M. Ketchum*

A steel engraving of Old Put taken from an 1862 volume with the snappy title NATIONAL PORTRAIT GALLERY OF EMINENT AMERICANS: INCLUDING ORATORS, STATESMEN, NAVAL AND MILITARY HEROES, JURISTS, AUTHORS, ETC., ETC., FROM ORIGINAL FULL-LENGTH PAINTINGS BY ALONZO CHAPPEL
COLLECTION OF OLIVER JENSEN

27

BEFORE
URBAN
RENEWAL

A visit to New York when it was

New York during the Revolution was, a loyalist wrote, "a most dirty, desolate and wretched place." And indeed it was. No other American city suffered as much from the war. It had been dug up by Americans for defense, shelled by British warships, ravaged by two severe fires, looted by enemy soldiers, even denuded of its trees for firewood. More than half its citizens had fled when the British began their seven-year occupation in the fall of 1776. Yet, astonishingly, by the turn of the century New York was on the threshold of becoming the largest city in the new Republic. By then it had already been—briefly, to be sure—both the nation's first capital and the capital of New York State. The number of its inhabitants had swollen from thirty-three thousand at the time of the first federal census in 1790 to sixty thousand in 1800 and to ninety-six thousand in 1810. Landfills joined new streets by the waterfront to the once-meandering cow paths of Dutch New Amsterdam. Spurred by the population growth, residents moved northward. In the spring of 1810 alone, more than six hundred stores and dwellings were being erected, and the next year the city fathers adopted a street system that led eventually to the later famous grid plan above the city's early settlements. It was during this spurt of activity that an obviously self-taught amateur painter named William Chappel did twenty-four known oil paintings of city life. On the back of each is a title or brief caption, but whether Chappel wrote them is not certain. Little is known about the artist, though one can surmise that he lived and worked on the Lower East Side, for his paintings are limited to scenes along the East River, in the Wall Street area and in what was called the Out Ward—sections of the city that were inhabited for the most part by laborers, shopkeepers, and tradesmen. But despite what little record he left of himself, Chappel did bequeath to us an image of New York as it once was, a city that, as an English visitor wrote in 1807, "is the finest and most agreeable...." —*N.B.*

Then and now: William Chappel's rendition of a house-raising on rural-seeming Grand Street in 1810 is framed by a photograph of how the site looks today.

little, not very old, and rather more attractive

EMMA LANDAU

VENDORS TO THE STREET TRADE

Top: A buttermilk "peddler" passes an old Dutch house on an unidentified street, 1807. Above: A baker's wagon on Hester Street in 1811 rolls by the shop of William Marshall, a potter who is hard at work by his window. The "Widow Bumstead" lives at the corner.

The "Old Watch House Wench" sells "Hot corn" at the intersection of the Bowery and Dover, Chatham, and Catharine streets, 1810. Situated near the Five Points area—later a hangout for notorious street gangs—this intersection today borders Chinatown.

A bootblack in 1808 plies his trade on Franklin Square, which looks much as it must have when Washington lived on it in 1789–90 in the home of Walter Franklin, a wealthy importer. The site of the house, not shown, now cushions a pier of the Brooklyn Bridge.

FOR EVERY NEED, A SERVICE

Chappel depicted the ferry slip at the foot of Chatham Street in 1808, when skiffs and rowboats were still used to reach Brooklyn.
Six years later a steam ferry made the run. In the background, right, is the Catharine Market, one of the city's six public markets.

Opposite, top: Ladder and lantern in tow, a lamplighter makes his rounds in 1806 on Broad Street, whose unusual width was due to the canal that once ran its course. Street lights used oil until 1825, when gas was introduced. Above: A night watchman leaves his "watchbox" to patrol snow-covered Elizabeth Street in 1809. Watchmen earned extra money for working in winter and for catching robbers. They were replaced by regular police officers in 1845.

Above left: Two chimney sweeps pause outside a coppersmith's shop on Cherry Street, 1810. Above: "The Dog Killer," his grisly chore done for a Water Street ship rigger named Davis, carries the victim away. Wild dogs had been a menace since Dutch days.

CITY LIFE—AND DEATH

Fly Market at Maiden Lane and Pearl Street, shown here in 1808, got its name from the Dutch vley, *"meadowland." Maiden Lane was "Maagde Paatje," a lovers' footpath. Pearl Street was named for the shells that lined its shore when it fronted on the river.*

Opposite, top: A baptism off Water Street on a Sunday morning in 1811. Above: The coffin of an infant is borne by eight girls to the Forsyth Street Methodist Episcopal Church. The chain across the street prevented traffic from disturbing the service.

Led by a drummer, a "Fat Cattle" (obviously a prize bovine, or why the flag it is sporting?) is paraded in an "Exhibition" near Bayard Street in 1809. The boot hanging from a pole at the corner house apparently indicates a cobbler in residence.

Defeated in his attempt at a political come-back in the Presidential election of 1912, the fifty-four-year-old Theodore Roosevelt started off 1913 eager for fresh adventures. The former President accepted invitations from the governments of Brazil, Argentina, and Chile to deliver addresses in their respective capitals and also gleefully agreed to accompany the explorer-priest John Augustine Zahm on a journey through the Amazon basin. The American Museum of Natural History in New York added two naturalists, George K. Cherrie and Leo E. Miller, to the party that would also include Roosevelt's second son, Kermit, who had been working for the past year and a half in Brazil. As well as being his father's beloved "side-partner," Kermit would prove invaluable as the expedition's interpreter and photographer. Some of his photographs taken during the trip appear in the following pages.

The story of T.R.'s extraordinary adventure in Brazil is told by Joseph L. Gardner in his new book, Departing Glory: Theodore Roosevelt as Ex-President, *from which this excerpt is taken. The book will be published this month by Charles Scribner's Sons. We pick up the story as the Roosevelt party boards the liner* Vandyck *in Brooklyn on October 4, 1913.*

For the sailing the ebullient T.R. wore a gray suit and a soft hat of the same color, a tie with a stick-pin, and a boutonniere in his lapel. The decks of the ship, the pier, and even a few surrounding streets were thronged with well-wishers; the Progressive (Bull Moose) Party sent a band; and the ambassadors of the three South American republics T.R. would visit came to see him off.

En route south the Colonel (as Roosevelt now liked to be called) easily proved to be the ship's most popular passenger. His uninhibited version of the sailor's hornpipe at an evening entertainment brought cries of "Encore," while George Cherrie noted that T.R.'s "two hundred and twenty pounds of avoirdupois were

the deciding factor in the 'tug-of-war' between the married men and the bachelors on the ship." A passenger who had originally said he would travel ten thousand miles to vote against Roosevelt was introduced to the ex-President, was charmed by him, and said that the next time he would travel twice as far to vote *for* him.

The first port of call on the cruise south was Bridgetown, Barbados, where the naturalist Leo Miller joined the party; and on October 17 the liner put in at Bahia, Brazil, where Kermit came aboard. Four days later the *Vandyck* steamed into Rio de Janeiro. A small fleet of gaily decked craft flying Brazilian and American flags welcomed the former President to the breathtakingly beautiful harbor; T.R.'s reception ashore,

wrote Father Zahm, had "all the wild enthusiasm of a national holiday."

At Rio, Roosevelt was met by Lauro Müller, the Brazilian minister of foreign affairs, who suggested a change in plans for his trip through the interior of the continent. At the headwaters of the Paraguay River, at the town of Cáceres, Roosevelt would be met by Colonel Candido Mariano da Silva Rondon, an army officer of chiefly Indian blood, who for the past quarter century had been exploring the Brazilian hinterland. Four years earlier, while surveying a route for a government telegraph line through the Mato Grosso, Colonel Rondon had come upon a large, previously unknown river flowing north. To this mysterious stream Rondon gave the name Rio da Dúvida, the "River of

AMERICAN HERITAGE BOOK SELECTION

T.R.'s
Last Adventure

By JOSEPH L. GARDNER

Doubt." Its course seemed to lie roughly along the parallel of longitude 60 degrees west of Greenwich, with a source between the 12th and 13th parallels south of the equator and perhaps an outlet into the Madeira, a major affluent of the Amazon. It was the largest uncharted river between the Gy-Paraná, another tributary to the Madeira, and the Juruena, which flowed into the Tapajós, yet another affluent of the Amazon. It was now Colonel Rondon's plan to follow the River of Doubt wherever it led, and Roosevelt was invited by the government to join him in this journey into the unknown.

T.R. knew that this was an unrivalled opportunity for another great adventure, his "last chance to be a boy"—and, of course, he accepted.

The undertaking was christened the Expedição Scientifica Roosevelt-Rondon; and while the Colonel completed his speaking tour Cherrie and Miller went up the Paraguay to begin collecting species of birds and mammals, and two other members of the party, Anthony Fiala and Jacob Sigg, organized the supplies.

By December 7 Roosevelt was at Asunción, the sleepy capital of the landlocked republic of Paraguay, and two days later he was journeying up the Paraguay River aboard the gunboat-yacht of the Paraguayan president. On the twelfth he reached the Brazilian boundary, where he was met by a shallow-draft river steamer carrying Colonel Rondon and his party. "Spick and span in their white uniforms," T.R. wrote of this initial meeting, the colonel and his companions came aboard Roosevelt's boat to introduce themselves. The Brazilian contingent would include four other officers, a doctor, and a geologist. "It was evident," T.R. noted of Rondon, "that he knew his business thoroughly, and it was equally evident that he would be a pleasant companion." T.R. spoke no Portuguese, and the officers apparently understood little English; but Kermit, after his year and a half in Brazil, could easily bridge the language gap.

During the next three weeks Roosevelt made a number of side trips to visit ranches and hunt jaguar, tapir, and the giant peccary—thus fulfilling his lifelong ambition to hunt the major big game of South America and also help complete the museum's collection of southern fauna. The indefatigable Colonel spent New Year's Day, January 1, 1914, on an all-day hunt on foot. Hacking their way through the thick jungle with machetes, wading through marshes up to their hips, swimming across two bayous, the members of the party were "drenched with sweat," wrote T.R., ". . . torn by the spines of the innumerable clusters of small pines with thorns like needles. . . . bitten by the hosts of fire-ants, and by the mosquitoes. . . ." T.R.'s watch, a veteran of Cuba, came to an "indignant halt," but he went on, although there was no breeze, the sun stood overhead in an "undimmed sky," and the "heat beat on us in waves." During these weeks Father Zahm described T.R. as being "happy as a schoolboy on a picnic."

En route up the Paraguay Roosevelt kept finding "so much of interest all along the banks that we were continually longing to stop and spend days where we were." He was utterly fascinated by the infinitely varied flora and fauna of Brazil and wrote knowingly and appreciatively of all he saw—especially the gorgeous birds. He seemed almost obsessed

Kermit catches his father and Father Zahm sharing a relaxed moment of conversation.

with the terrifying piranha fish and eagerly collected accounts of their grisly proclivities. Almost every night he would work at the magazine articles that *Scribner's Magazine* had commissioned him to write about the expedition. When other members of the party would flop wearily into their hammocks, he would sit at his folding table, his head draped in mosquito netting, his hands and arms protected from the insects by thick gloves and gauntlets, slowly writing out in longhand these articles, later published in book form as *Through the Brazilian Wilderness*. Until they reached the headwaters of the River of Doubt, the finished pieces could still be sent back to New York for publication. But he continued to work on the articles after the expedition plunged into the unknown, even working when he was tormented with a fever. "This is not written very clearly," he advised his editor at *Scribner's* in the margin of one manuscript; "my temperature is 105."

T.R. had brought no books with him on this trip, and for his reading he had to fall back on Kermit's *Oxford Book of French Verse* and Everyman editions of Gibbon and Epictetus. Kermit had also brought a few French novels, which T.R. disdained.

On January 15 the party reached the outpost of Tapirapuan on an upper tributary of the Paraguay, and there they left their boats. All the specimens thus far gathered, along with all baggage no longer deemed essential, were sent back down the river and eventually to New York. Six days later the expedition took off on horse and mule for a month-long trek across the highland wilderness of the Mato Grosso—a "healthy land of dry air, of cool nights, of clear, running brooks," T.R. called it. Father Zahm did not find the terrain quite so enticing; rarely did they see a tree more than twenty feet high, and the lack of water became a serious problem for the animals. Soon, along the route they were following, they began

to see carcasses and bleaching bones of pack animals from the supply train that had been sent on ahead. Ominously, among the bones were abandoned boxes labelled "Roosevelt South American Expedition." With muleteers, cooks, and other assistants the expedition now numbered nearly forty persons; there were some two hundred pack animals. So impressive was the train that Fiala recorded its departure from Tapirapuan on motion-picture film. The third day out the expedition crossed the divide separating the basin of the Paraguay from that of the Amazon, and for this part of the journey they could follow the telegraph lines set up along the route surveyed a few years earlier by Colonel Rondon.

By February 1 the expedition was at Utiarity, an Indian settlement and telegraph station on the Rio Papagaio. From this point Father Zahm—who had decided against making the exploration of the Rio da Dúvida with Roosevelt—and Sigg returned to civilization, while Fiala and one of the Brazilian officers departed for a canoe trip down the Juruena and Tapajós to the Amazon. The main body continued overland to the headwaters of the Dúvida, which was reached on February 26. Here the final separation was made. Miller, with two officers and the geologist, was to march three days to the Gy-Paraná and follow it down to the Madeira and eventually the Amazon, a route previously explored by Rondon. Unless they encountered the others, coming down the Dúvida to its supposed juncture with the Madeira, they were to proceed to Manáos for an eventual rendezvous.

Shortly after noon on February 27 the Gy-Paraná group gathered on the fragile wooden bridge that had been flung across the Rio da Dúvida at the telegraph-line crossing to wave good-bye and call out "Good Luck" to the Roosevelt-Rondon party. In addition to the two colonels the exploring

team included Kermit, Cherrie, a Lieutenant Lyra, Doctor Cajazeira, and sixteen *camaradas,* the expert rivermen of the tropical forest. The paddlers, T.R. wrote, were "a strapping set. . . . lithe as panthers and brawny as bears." They swam like water dogs, he reported, and "were equally at home with pole and paddle, with axe and machete." The *camaradas* looked like pirates out of a storybook, he further noted; indeed, "one or two of them were pirates, and one worse than a pirate." They were white, black, copper-colored, "and of all intermediate shades"; of Portuguese, Negro, and Indian blood. As a group they were "hard-working, willing, and cheerful."

The twenty-two-man party would travel in seven dugout canoes—one small, one "cranky," two "old, water-logged, and leaky," three good. Personal baggage had been cut down to the "limit necessary for health and efficiency"; yet in such a voyage it was impossible not to take a large amount of equipment, and the canoes, Roosevelt later wrote, were too heavily laden.

The Colonel, Cherrie, and Kermit would share a light tent; the three Brazilian officers would have another tent; and there would be a third for anyone who felt sick. The *camaradas* would sleep in hammocks slung between trees. All would be armed, but shooting would only be permitted for collecting species, procuring food, and warning off or repelling Indian attacks. The food and arms taken "represented all reasonable precautions against suffering and starvation"; there were provisions for fifty days but "not full rations, for we hoped in part to live on the country—on fish, game, nuts, and palm tops." Yet, the Colonel conceded, anything might happen: "We were about to go into the unknown, and no one could say what it held."

The surveying was to be done by Colonel Rondon and Lieutenant Lyra, assisted by Kermit. The

CONTINUED ON PAGE 79

Through the Brazilian Wilderness, BY
THEODORE ROOSEVELT (SCRIBNER'S, 1914)

Three stages of their journey down the River of Doubt are recorded in Kermit's pictures. First, as T.R. wrote, the river was a "placid stream."

Fear of Indians, plus millions of mosquitoes, made camping at night nerve-racking, but T.R.—seen here at right—was unfailingly cheerful.

They were repeatedly confronted with the grueling job of portaging the dugouts around perilous rapids. Logs were used as rollers under the canoes.

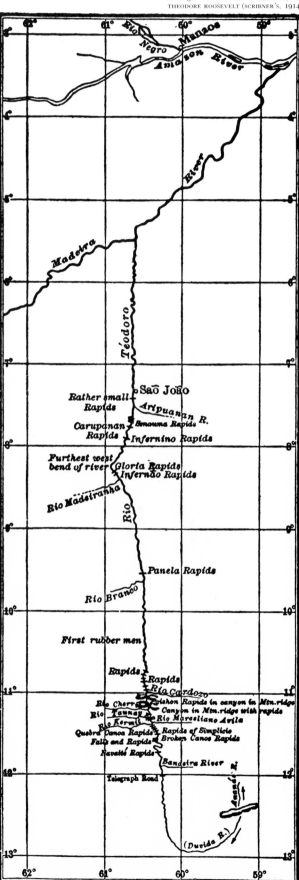

This sketch-map of the Rio Téodoro—as the Rio Roosevelt is sometimes called—was drafted by Roosevelt from his journal.

An Artist in America

By ROBERT S. GALLAGHER

Thomas Hart Benton, one of the nation's premier muralists, was born in Neosho, Missouri, on April 15, 1889, and was named for his famous great-uncle, who became a political legend during three decades of service as that state's first U.S. senator. The elder Thomas Hart Benton (1782–1858) migrated out of common sense to the Missouri Territory in 1815 partly because of a notorious and bloody brawl in Tennessee with Andrew Jackson. [See "Now defend yourself, you damned rascal!" AMERICAN HERITAGE, *February, 1958.] In 1907 his namesake abandoned Missouri and the Benton family tradition of a career in law and politics. He enrolled at the Art Institute of Chicago, departing a year later for Paris, where he studied at the Académie Julian until 1911. The years just before World War I he spent in New York City experimenting with the various postimpressionist theories of art that emanated with bewildering rapidity from France. After a wartime stint in the Navy Benton returned to New York, where he worked as an instructor at the Art Students League and gradually acquired a reputation as a promising contemporary muralist. This led to his first important assignment, at the New School for Social Research (1931), followed by mural commissions from the Whitney Museum of American Art (1932), the Indiana exhibit at the Century of Progress Exposition in Chicago (1933), and the Missouri State House (1936) in Jefferson City. His painting invariably involved him in stormy controversy with radical and conservative critics alike, but his explicit style and use of nativist subject matter soon brought him recognition, along with Grant Wood and John Steuart Curry, as a leader of the regionalist movement. In 1935 he joined the faculty of the Art Institute in Kansas City, Missouri, where he still maintains his home and studio. His autobiography,* An Artist in America, *was first published in 1937 and has since gone through two revisions and numerous printings. Still active at the easel, he retired from mural work in 1961 after completing his Truman Library project in Independence, but he returned to this medium last spring to help Joplin, Missouri, where he got his start as an artist, celebrate its centennial. Since 1920 Benton has summered on Martha's Vineyard off Cape Cod with his wife, Rita, and their two children. There, at his three-room shingled cottage on a windswept*

bluff at Gay Head, he recently interrupted his construction of a stone sea wall to discuss his turbulent career.

* * * * *

Being named Thomas Hart Benton in Missouri must have been like being named Daniel Webster in Massachusetts.

Very likely 'tis. It was a family name, and I was the first male in my immediate family born in Missouri, and it was quite natural to name me after the first of my line to come to Missouri. There are two lines of Bentons, one Yankee and one southern. I'm southern.

Do you think your name may have impelled you to fame?

No, I would not believe that at all. I've never had any strong feeling that I have to emulate any ancestor. I wasn't aware of the implications of the name at first, of course. I became aware of it quick enough, because that was drilled into me. I was also raised with a certain view of American history. From the time I was five years old I was got into the habit of reading and listening to it. That was all part of my father's effort to make me a lawyer.

What did your father, Colonel M. E. Benton . . . incidentally, what did the M stand for?

Maecenas—M-A-E-C-E-N-A-S. He was the great Roman protector of the arts, which my father was not.

Your father was a lawyer, wasn't he?

My father was a lawyer who rose to political power in Missouri after a fracas with President Grover Cleveland. He was then the U.S. attorney for the western district of Missouri, and Cleveland suspended him from office for what was called offensive partisanship. But his suspen-

Thomas Hart Benton, photographed at his summer home on Martha's Vineyard, 1972

sion raised such a stink that he was promptly put back in. He was attached to the Populist movement that was led in Missouri by Senator George Fisk, and my father rode that Populist vote into power.

And into Congress?

Yes, he served in the House from 1897 until 1905. I guess you could say that the core of our family life was politics. Many of my earliest memories are of the politicians who came to dinner at our house, men like Champ Clark and William Jennings Bryan, big men with huge cigars and larger appetites. And when my father went out campaigning, I went along. By the time I was ten, I knew all about the political rallies and camp meetings and backwoods hotels. It was a much different style than we have today. I'll say one thing, though. It forced a man into much closer relations with his constituents than he need have today.

Did living in the nation's capital as a boy have any effect on the direction of your life?

Had we remained in the little town of Neosho, I don't know whether I would have had the early training that made it possible for me, at seventeen, to take up a professional job as an artist. But in Washington, both in the grade schools and in high school, my drawing was encouraged. I also spent a lot of time imitating a Washington cartoonist named Berryman. His style of crosshatching fascinated me, and when my father would take me up to the House, I'd sit there for hours sketching the congressmen, especially Uncle Joe Cannon, the famous Speaker. I'll bet I drew him a hundred times.

It sounds as if you enjoyed your years in Washington.

You live in a city like Washington, even as a boy of fourteen or so, and you learn more about life than any school has to teach you. We lived a few doors from the Chinese embassy, and that was a fascinating damned place to hang around. And as a congressman's son I had access to the shelves of the Library of Congress, and there I ran into Burton's translation of the tales of the *Arabian Nights*, and for a kid, that was highly seductive stuff, let me tell you. I still read it, twenty-four volumes, footnotes and all, and when I get to the end, I start again because I've forgotten the language of the first part. I've done that for years and years.

At first drawing was just a hobby with you?

Until I was seventeen, yes. That was when I broke up my father's plan to make a lawyer out of me, and the break was accidental. I was working up in Joplin with my cousin's surveying outfit, and one Saturday night I wandered into the town's main saloon, the House of Lords, to have a beer. Well, over the bar was a huge painting of a masked nude, which, as you can imagine, I got to studying pretty intently. The next thing I knew, a bunch of miners and roughnecks started kidding me with a barrage of obscene suggestions. I was so embarrassed that, in desperation, I started insisting that the reason I was looking at the picture was that I was a professional artist. Well, one of those hecklers happened to know that the local paper needed an artist, and he decided to call my bluff, so the first thing I knew we were on our way over to the offices of the Joplin *American*. As a test the editor had me go make a sketch of a local druggist, and I got the job at fourteen dollars a week. Once I got that job, I didn't want to go back to monkeying with the law. Besides, there weren't any law clerks in that part of the country making fourteen dollars a week, and my father knew that, and he knew *I* knew it, too. He gave in finally, and sent me to art school in Chicago, but he was very much disappointed.

H*ow old were you when you moved on to study in Paris?*

That was in 1909, and I was just nineteen. It was exciting and very highly stimulating for a young man, perhaps too stimulating for someone so young. The Paris of my time was really the beginning of all these colossal nervous changes in the art world. What was good one year, two years later you were doubtful about. Of course, today it's next week you're doubtful about it.

Paris left you confused as an artist?

There was too much ferment, too many directions all competing for the attention of the artist. And it was also a very lonely time for me. You see, I was too young for the café crowd. As I look back on it I don't think it's good psychologically for a young man to be that alone all the time, or alone with some damned woman to dominate you, which generally comes up, you know, when you're that alone.

You once described Paris as the "usual story"—a mistress, a studio, some work, and lots of talk.

I haven't written too much about those days because, well, so many of the people involved, or their children, are still around. But it's true, a mistress was generally accepted practice, and when you left, you left her what money you had, what furniture you had, and she hunted around for another artist. Most of those girls, I guess you could say, were very effective as "caretakers of the young."

What finally made you leave Paris and return to this country?

Well, one day my mother and sister arrived unexpectedly to visit me, although I don't particularly want to elaborate on that. Naturally, when a young fellow gets set up with a life of his own, he doesn't want the interference of his family. I ran around making new arrangements as fast as I could, but of course they weren't enough to disguise the situation.

What was your mother's reaction?

It was the natural reaction of any mother who finds her son with a new woman dominating the situation.

Was that what prompted your parents to discontinue supporting your art study abroad?

I'll tell you the truth about that. When I was a little boy, one of my uncles bequeathed me $3,500 for my education, which was a sizable sum in those days. And frankly, that did the business, all through my study in Chicago and my three years in Paris. Now you couldn't do that today. My daughter, Jessie, cost more than that per year in Radcliffe.

In your various writings about this period, you seem to show a decided aversion to formal art training.

That's true. And I'll tell you, since you've caught that by implication, that even in the modern art formulas I had the same distrust, and that's why I never attached myself for very long to any of the modern movements, although I experimented with a good many of them.

Do you think your Populist background has anything to do with that distrust?

Yes. There has always been a slight resentment in me for any institutionalized forms of art, whether they are radical or conservative.

But do you see any direct parallels between political Populism and the form and content of your art?

People have seen such a connection, not just in the very strong strain of anti-intellectualism, but, well, it's almost anticapitalism or antisociety as it was instituted at the time of the rise of Populism. Populism was a revolt of the farmers against the control of the market, against the rise of the promoter and the entrepreneur over the producer. This was something like the way I've felt toward the whole art establishment, yes, be it radical or conservative. I never got along with either of them. I made some effort, especially toward the modernists. But my art after 1920, and certainly after 1925, turned increasingly back toward the subject matter of my youth. Just the same, you want to understand here, my point of view has been exaggerated. I have never been totally negative about modern art, although I must say that back in my early days in Paris, even before the rise of cubism, it was a common belief among critics and even many artists, like my friend Leo Stein, that the disintegration of art would eventually lead, as it has, to an empty square of canvas.

Like the painting of Mark Rothko?

And many others before him. He was the one that became well-known for it.

During your early, developmental years in New York, how did you support yourself?

One of the ways I managed it came about through a friend, Rex Ingram, who was a director in the film industry's early days in Fort Lee, New Jersey. He got me involved in 1914 as a set designer and general handyman, at seven and a half dollars a day. I worked for, I believe it was Pathé at first, and later with Fox. I had five years' experience with it, off and on. It was all very informal in those days, and the pictures were just sort of made up as they went along. I recall how the workmen, the designer, the head scene-painter, and myself would have dinner at Lüchow's to plan what we were going to do the next day. Then I would go over to the New York Public Library and look up what I could on the background of whatever the story called for. Then I would make sketches and go back to the film studio, where I would paint—everything was in black and white, of course—the backdrops, which were quite illusionary.

Did you ever work with any of the big stars of that period, like Valentino?

I met him, I didn't know him. I worked, now that I think of it, on the early planning of *The Four Horsemen of the Apocalypse*, and the cape that Valentino wore in that movie and the cane that he carried were mine. I had brought them back from Paris.

Did you ever do any more work for the motion-picture industry?

You mean on films? Yes. Walt Disney brought me out to Hollywood in 1946 to work on a picture that would have been sort of an American operetta about the life of Davy Crockett. Well, Disney had just put up a huge modern studio and was tremendously overextended financially, and his operations were actually under the control of a big New York City bank. And immediately the bankers started meddling with the story line. They knew that a large percentage of Disney's profits came from showing his films in Latin America, and so they didn't think it would be good business to have Crockett killed at the Alamo by Mexicans. So I suggested that we have Davy die in Congress from listening to all the oratory. They didn't like that, of course. They wanted him to just fade gloriously up in the sky or something. Well, hell, I wasn't going to have any part of that, so I sold my interest in the project to Disney for three thousand dollars and went home. I wish I hadn't signed away my interest. Years later Walt put Crockett on television and made a fortune.

During the period before World War I you were part of the group that frequented the studio of Alfred Stieglitz and congregated at the old Lincoln Square Arcade at Sixty-fifth and Broadway. Wasn't it in the Arcade that you were once stabbed by a girl friend?

Uh-huh. . . . Well, you see, fractions occur among the young, and I guess I made this girl mad, I don't know over what. Actually, she surprised me. She'd have never gotten close enough to cut me if I had thought she was mad. The fact is that creative people attract women, for some god-damned reason. Wherever you find a bunch of artists, there's always a bunch of women. I'm tempted to say that the female in our society has not been generally so economically conditioned as the male, and I believe that women are simply attracted to the sort of basic human things that an artist must deal with. But remember, these are special women, all of whom are themselves engaged in some artistic line.

I suppose one of the most significant things that occurred during this period of your life was the 1913 Armory Show in New York?

I missed it. My mother had taken sick, and my father thought I should come home to Missouri, so I didn't see the show. But I soon saw what its effects were, and I participated myself in the next modern show.

That would be the 1916 Forum Show staged by the synchromists?

Yeah. You see, the bigger part of the critical response to the 1913 show was adverse, although the younger critics, they swallowed it whole. I know in the past I've said

that show might have been detrimental to the growth of American art, but today I think it was a good idea that these new idioms were injected into the American scene, because we are, after all, an outlying part of European civilization, and it was therefore almost unavoidable that these new idioms should come in. As far as the larger question of how important the modernist movement really is, well, it will take us another fifty or sixty years to judge that.

When this country went to war in 1917, you enlisted in the Navy. You once explained that by saying you didn't want "to interfere with the progress of any German bullets."

I used political influence to get into the Navy. The U.S. Postmaster General was Governor Dockery of Missouri, a close friend of my father's, and the governor was in sympathy with the German element in Missouri who didn't want to be in the war, too. It was that simple. You see, we all believed that it was simply a war between the big capitalist nations for control of the world's resources. And largely that's what it was.

W*as your art affected by your Navy experience?*

It certainly was. I worked a good part of the time as a draftsman, and that had a lot to do with my return to representational art. But what was equally important about this period was that I began reading American history again.

Then you consider your study of American history an important influence in your career?

Of course. That and having been introduced in Paris to the ideas set forth by Hippolyte Taine in his *Philosophie de l'Art.* Taine would not accept the modernist argument that art had a separate existence from society, and neither do I. Well, at any rate, after I got out of the Navy, I set to work on a series of paintings about American history, and I worked on that project from about 1920 to 1926. Originally, I planned to paint ten "chapters" of five paintings each, which would depict the history of the country from its settlement to the 1920's, but I only finished the first two chapters. These were exhibited, as I completed them, at the annual shows of the Architectural League in New York, and through them I gradually became known as a muralist. And during the same period, I executed my first genre paintings of American life during summer visits here at Martha's Vineyard.

TEXT CONTINUES ON PAGE 48

Benton's Missouri Mural

Three of the four walls of the House lounge, on the third floor of Missouri's splendid capitol in Jefferson City, present the mural painting that Thomas Hart Benton regards as his best work. The subject is, of course, the history and folklore of Missouri. Benton's interpretation is generic for the most part: although some specific characters can be recognized (as in the panel over the door, above, showing Huck Finn and Jim on their Mississippi raft), the artist's intention was to paint a series of typical Missouri scenes enacted by typical Missouri people. The style is mature Benton, strong in color and sinewy in line; he completed the work in 1936 when he had reached the height of his career. Not everybody liked it, however. "There were some State Representatives who thought the mural ought to be whitewashed off the wall after I had finished it," Benton once said. "I figured that by the time they got the votes to do the whitewashing, they'd probably get to liking the mural. They did!" For additional views of the mural, plus other samples of Benton's work, turn the page.

Benton has always had a sharp appreciation of regional types: he used "Missouri people that I met and knew" as his models for the whole mural.

While celebrating the homespun texture of Missouri life in general, Benton managed to work in a few specific allusions: the politician for whom the campaign meeting above left is being held is the famous Champ Clark, U.S. congressman from Missouri for over a quarter of a century (1893–95, 1897–1921); the notorious Thomas Joseph "Boss" Pendergast of Kansas City is seen opposite, far right, enjoying a cigar.

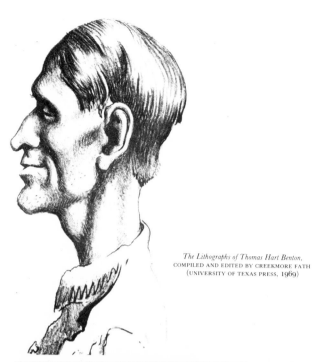

The Lithographs of Thomas Hart Benton,
COMPILED AND EDITED BY CREEKMORE FATH
(UNIVERSITY OF TEXAS PRESS, 1969)

*Jesse James (opposite) and Frankie and Johnny (above) were three
semimythical figures commemorated in panels of the State House mural.
Three separately done lithographs illustrate Benton's treatment of faces.*

Did your marriage to Rita Piacenza in 1922 change your career?

I think it did. It made me a damned sight more peaceful. As a matter of fact, since 1948 she's handled practically all the business. She's a very good salesman, and it has been through Rita that I have actually been able to keep up competition with the New York dealers so that they'll pay my prices. And she was very important in the beginning, too, in that she earned a good deal through her work in the fashion field. Then there was Dr. Alfred Raabe.

Who was he?

Raabe was a Ukrainian who immigrated to this country and started practicing medicine in the Bronx. He just had an interest in the arts, and by chance he ran into me, and we liked each other. He'd come around to my studio every so often and collect a batch of my paintings and sketches. He'd put frames on them—it was a hobby of his—and then he'd hang them in his patients' bedrooms. He must have sold hundreds of them to his patients, at very low prices. But I want to say something about that. Never, even when I became well-known and my pictures started bringing good prices, never have those paintings come on the market. I consider that quite a tribute.

When *did you make your first important sale?*

It was in 1922 at an exhibition at the old Pennsylvania Academy of Art in Philadelphia. The purchaser was an eccentric patent-medicine manufacturer and art collector named Albert Barnes, and having Barnes buy one of my paintings was a great help to my reputation. Later, I helped him with a book on the arts that he wanted to write, but we didn't agree very long.

Did Barnes ever send you one of his celebrated letters?

Oh, hell yes. Everybody got one. You know, Barnes was also an amateur psychologist, and he could really be devastating. Briefly, what he said was that my cockiness with regard to the arts derived from the fact that I was only a runt anyhow, and runts like me are always combative. He was a vicious bastard, but he did love art.

Is there any particular moment or period in your life that you would consider a crucial turning point?

Well, if there was one, it was probably in 1924. My father had a cancer and was dying, and I went out to Spring-

field, Missouri, to sort of take care of him. While I was there I began to meet people I'd known, and in interim moments I went with my brother down in the Ozarks to see if that life I knew in my youth still existed. I guess that got me started walking around the rural parts of the South and West, sketching the people and joining in their revival meetings and helping them drink their moonshine. Some of my walking tours over the next decade, like the one I made through the Smokies, were prolonged, often lasting two or three months. Those areas were still full of adventure in those days, and some of it, like the time the coal-mine police confiscated my sketchbooks and chased me clear into the next county, got a little hair-raising. But I got along fine with the common folk, who weren't as suspicious of outsiders then as they are now. I kept extensive notes on my adventures, and in 1934 I put it all down in a sort of autobiography called *An Artist in America*.

For a painter, you've certainly published a lot.

I suppose I enjoy writing, although at times it can be very annoying, and, as you know, the critics don't like artists to be articulate.

Why is that?

The critics, quite frankly, prefer that artists don't speak for themselves. They prefer a guy like Jackson Pollock, who was completely inarticulate. That way the critics have perfect freedom to say anything they like.

You don't have a very high opinion of art critics, do you?

Well, there are different kinds of critics. I know certain scholars who might be called critics, and these men, like Ruskin and Taine, can be of immense value to you. You see, you may not believe in Plato's ideas of art, but they *are* ideas, and very important. But you don't ever get any ideas from the average critic, just fancy writing and a lot of trivial, personal observations.

In your book, the people you met on your walking tours all seem so, well, unaffected. Is it possible your view might have been somewhat romanticized?

Possibly. Certainly after 1926 these travels were an attempt to recapture the sectional culture of my youth. And possibly any of my art that pictured that would have the character of a romance. Perhaps I had a romantic view of it. That isn't a bad word at all, in my estimation.

Do you think most parts of America are losing their sectional flavor today?

CONTINUED ON PAGE 85

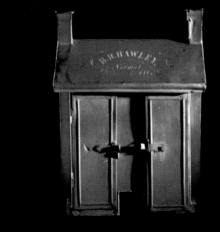

VANISHING HERITAGE

A careless America has lost or ignored most of its priceless collection of patent models. Sometimes exquisite, sometimes little more than toys, those that remain display in the inventors' own handiwork the history of our technology

Portfolio photographed by
William R. Ray
For an explanation of the
models on this page see page 63.

The engaging artifacts on the preceding page are, for all their quiet simplicity, survivors of an extraordinarily harrowing career. More important, they are part of a national treasure that is now threatened and dwindling almost daily. They are patent models, and each of them is a small monument to the native genius for invention that has put its stamp on all our national development.

The models go back to the earliest days of the Republic. While the thirteen states were still coping with the ratification of the Constitution, Secretary of State Thomas Jefferson, together with Henry Knox and Edmund Randolph, formed the Patent Commission. George Washington signed their bill, and for the first time in history the right of an inventor to profit from his invention was recognized by law instead of an occasional royal whim. From the very first an inventor who applied for a patent was required to submit not only a drawing of his invention but also a model to show how it worked. This Jeffersonian stipulation remained in effect for eighty years and caused chaotic difficulties from the beginning.

The models came into Washington in such unexpected quantity that by 1810 Congress had to appropriate funds to purchase Blodgett's Hotel—actually an old theatre—for storage and display space. The local citizenry took to touring the building on Sundays and admiring the products of Yankee ingenuity.

The first of many threats came to the models four years later when the British burned Washington. Dr. William Thornton, superintendent of the Patent Office, had fled the city but returned when he learned that Blodgett's was endangered. He accosted a British colonel whose men were about to put it to the torch and with desperate, high-flown rhetoric compared his imminent burning of the models to the Turkish destruction of the library at Alexandria. The colonel was won over, and Blodgett's was spared from the flames.

Thornton's eloquence was the high-water mark of the government's concern for its patent models, and the rest of their history is a catalogue of disasters. In 1836 all the collection of seven thousand models was lost when a fire levelled Blodgett's.

A fine new patent office with vast east and west wings was designed and built, but the enormous influx of new models prevented proper cataloguing and storage. In 1870 a new law made the submission of models discretionary with the commissioner of patents, but the models kept coming in. Ten years later the stipulation was dropped completely, with the major exception of patents for flying machines. This last requirement was waived after the Wright brothers coaxed their biplane into the air in 1903, but the Patent Office still prudently demands a working model before it will issue a patent for a perpetual-motion machine.

With the flood of incoming models stopped, space still had to be found for well over 200,000 already on hand. Another fire tragically disposed of 76,000 of them in 1877, and the rest were eventually moved to a warehouse. In 1908 Congress decided to have done with the bulky things and offered them all for sale, having first given the Smithsonian Institution the chance to cull out some of the most interesting for their collections. Three thousand models brought in a forlorn total of $62.18 on the block. Some eight hundred of those have wound up safely in the Hagley Museum, part of the Du Pont museum complex in Wilmington, Delaware. The rest—155,939 of them—began a dreary round of moving from one storage dump to another. They passed through such unlikely depositories as a basement under the House of Representatives and the District of Columbia's Male Work House and finally came to rest in an abandoned livery stable.

Here amid the pungent odors and empty stalls they stayed until 1926, when Sir Henry Wellcome—a British subject, ironically, and head of a hugely successful drug-manufacturing corporation—bought up the whole lot, probably with the idea of starting a museum. After his death his estate sold them to a Broadway producer who whipped up enough press coverage to resell them at a good profit to a group of businessmen. They had even less luck, and by 1941 the models were in a warehouse in New Rochelle, New York.

At this time their current owner, O. Rundle Gilbert, an auctioneer, got together some partners and bought up the lot for a mere $2,100, plus the accumulated storage bills of more than $11,000. The only other bidder was a man interested in selling the models to Japan for their scrap value. The models made a trip up to Garrison, New York, where they remain today in Gilbert's barns.

Gilbert, too, had hoped to establish a museum, but after years of expenditures with no returns he has recently been selling the models piecemeal at shows and auctions for as little as twenty-five dollars. The vast majority, however, are still in his barn packed in unidentified crates that have not been opened for more than a half century.

As the pictures on the following pages show, the models deserve far more recognition than they have received. They are delightful and important relics. Some are wonders of complexity, and some are clumsy and primitive expressions of simple, lost ideas. The history of America has always been a history of experiment and invention. The men who met in Philadelphia during the sweltering summer of 1776 to experiment with an untried form of government are allied in spirit with the legion of inventors, known and unknown, who came after and met the challenges of their land and their era with ingenuity. They have left us a bright and intricate legacy. The models that they submitted in hopes of fame or of the sudden fortune that other men had enjoyed in the new country speak eloquently of both hardships and genius. Some are of towering importance, and some ludicrous in their triviality, but all are singularly American works of art. Could not a free-spending Congress, always willing to appropriate the seven million dollars needed for every mile of superhighway, buy the models back before they are permanently dispersed? The $13,000-odd that Gilbert paid for his lot would build less than ten feet of interstate.

—*Richard F. Snow*

Reuben Spalding's flying machine of 1889 embodies the aspiration and folly reflected in many patent models. The aeronaut would have hung and flapped under a small balloon.

William R. Ray, former Life photographer, and his wife, Marlys, have prepared a book on patent models entitled The Art of Invention, to be published by the Pyne Press, Princeton, New Jersey.

ABE LINCOLN HAD AN IDEA

"The Patent System added the fuel of interest to the fire of genius," wrote Abraham Lincoln. He had good reason to know the workings of the system, for in 1849 he was awarded Patent No. 6,469 for "A Device for Buoying Vessels over Shoals." Lincoln, no stranger to the perils of river travel, was twice aboard boats that ran aground. The model of his solution for such mishaps appears above. The "buoyant chambers" along the hull are inflated with air to refloat the stranded ship. Lincoln never profited from his idea, but he did carry his interest in inventions into the White House, with important consequences. It was only Lincoln's vigorous support of John Ericcson that enabled the Swedish inventor to finish the *Monitor* in time for her fateful appointment with the Confederate ironclad *Merrimac.*

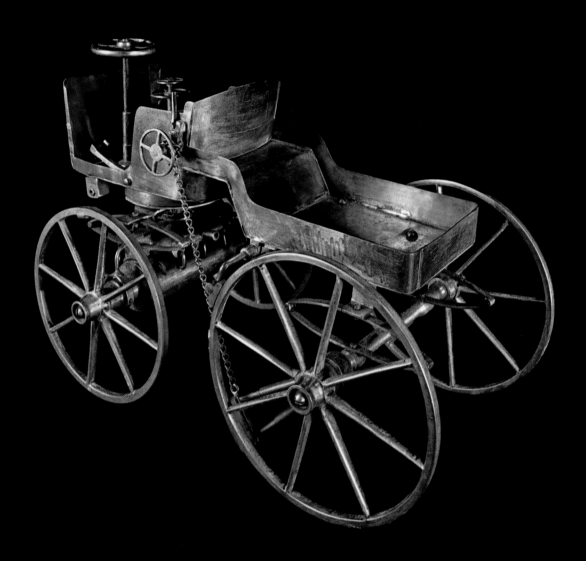

GEORGE SELDEN LOST A MONOPOLY

The pretty little brass toy above was the focus of one of the most complex and costly court battles ever fought. It is the model that George Selden submitted for an automobile patent granted in 1895 which, he later claimed, covered all internal-combustion cars produced by the infant industry. Henry Ford thought differently and refused to pay the royalty that Selden's company demanded on every car sold. In 1911, after years of litigation, the court decided in favor of Ford and the other manufacturers that had stood against Selden. The court held that Selden's cars relied on the two-stroke Brayton engine of 1874—the model to the far right. The motor companies, however, were using the more sophisticated four-stroke Otto engine of 1877, which is shown next to Brayton's.

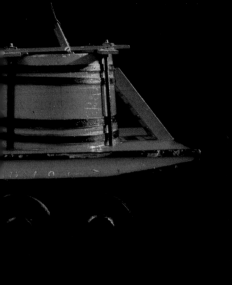

The railroad played an enormous role in nineteenth-century America, and it is not surprising that many of the models represent various aspects of its development. The selection on these pages also shows the vast range in quality of the patent models. They had only to show how the invention worked; any further embellishments were added at the whim of the builder. The contrast is particularly striking between the beautifully finished sculpture at the lower left of the page and the crude tin construction directly above it. Here, clockwise from the upper left, are models of an 1850 improvement for engines working steep grades; a car of 1866 for carrying oil; a device for sanding rails in icy weather (the sand is discharged from the pipe ahead of the front driving wheel); a smokestack extension to keep cinders off the passengers; Samuel Vauclain's compound engine valve of 1889; and a heating and ventilation system for passenger cars

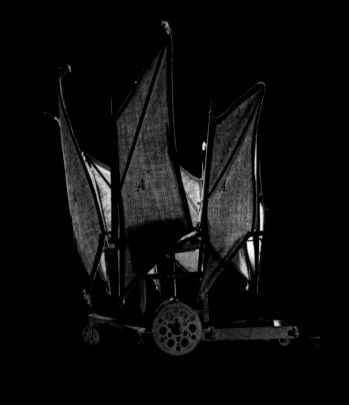

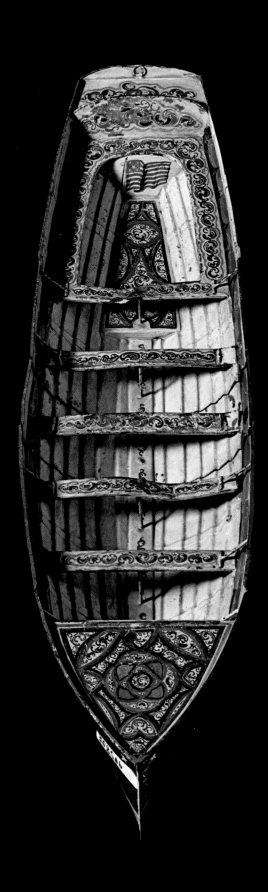

PRACTICAL NAVIGATION

Abraham Lincoln was only one of scores of inventors who were granted patents for nautical innovations. River commerce was as important as the railroad to the economic life of America, and with one exception the models on these pages are the handiwork of men who strove to make travel by water safer and easier. The exception is the curious machine in the upper left-hand corner, a "Wind-Engine" patented by John Cook in 1878. It is shown here attached to a plow, but Cook optimistically suggested that it could also be used to drive almost anything. Next to the Wind-Engine is an 1872 device for raising and lowering steamboat stacks. Steamboat companies often complained that bridges blocked their right of way. The split funnel of 1872 offered a solution to the problem and has enjoyed general use ever since. Above is an elaborate lifeboat, with the chamber for the crew hung on pinions in order to compensate for the motion of the vessel. The intricately painted craft to the right is the model of an 1858 patent for metal boats. The steamboat to the left demonstrates an 1853 idea for an improved steering mechanism. As in the case of the colorful 4-4-0 locomotive on the preceding page, the inventor went far beyond the basic necessity of demonstrating the workings of his patent and produced a most engaging and whimsical bit of folk art.

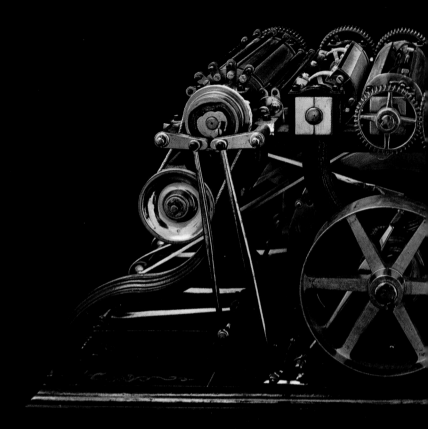

Joseph Firmenich
and
Flavius P. Stibe
of
Buffalo, N.Y.
Improved
Steam Boiler.

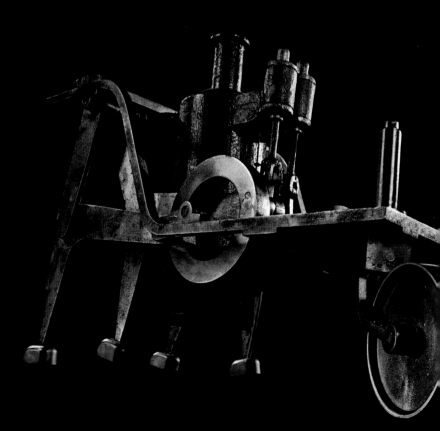

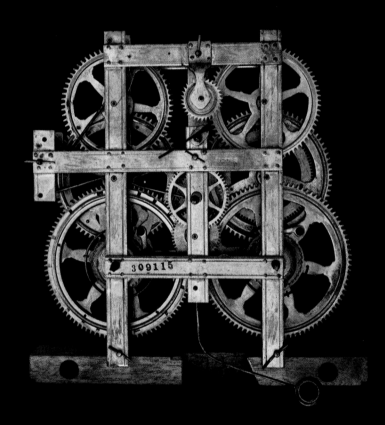

INDUSTRIES IN MINIATURE

Inventors met the demands of our burgeoning technology with a diversity of ideas, some foolish, some of lasting importance. The marvelously complex model above represents a rotary press patented by William Bullock in 1863, which incorporates features that are still in use. To the right of the press is a clockwork from 1833, and below it a machine invented in 1878 by John H. Heinz to sort vegetables for some of his 57 varieties. The eerily anthropomorphic juggernaut, below left, is a traction engine designed to walk on iron legs. John E. Praul, who patented it in 1879, has long been forgotten. Not so Thomas Edison, who created the "Printing-Telegraph" at the lower left in 1873. The boiler at left center was patented in 1875. Above it is a metal shearer brightly painted by the inventor in hopes, perhaps, of beguiling the patent inspector.

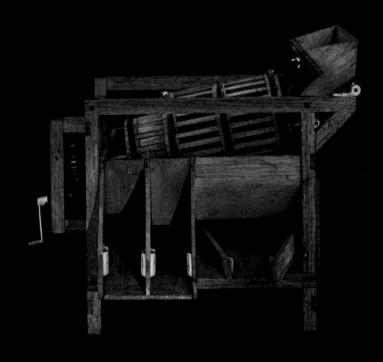

DOMESTIC GENIUS

The home life of Americans also bene-
fited from the inventors' zeal, as the
models on these pages attest. Undoubtedly the most important is Isaac
Singer's sewing machine of 1851, in
the center at far right. Singer was already in production when he submitted
his model; it is a working machine,
bearing the serial number 22. The
highly ornamental sewing machine to
its left, with its gilded mermaid and
classical figures, was submitted for a
design—rather than a mechanical—
patent in 1859. However, the inventor
of the third sewing machine (to the
left of this text) was interested only in
patenting its chain-stitch mechanism
and freely gave his elegant dolphin
design of 1855 to the world. Cutting's
clothes-drier on the upper right still
bears the tag that the Patent Office
used to affix to all models. The wide-
mouthed visage at the lower right
conceals an elaborate animal trap.
William Weaver offered the oddly
streamlined machine at left center as
an example of his improved cherry-
stoner. Clothespins have not changed a
great deal, over the years, from most
of the models shown above, but the
spindly relic to the left of them is barely recognizable today as a radiator.

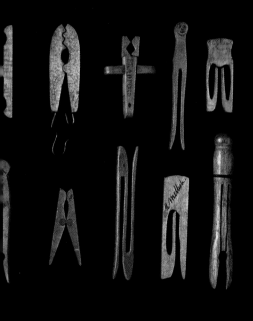

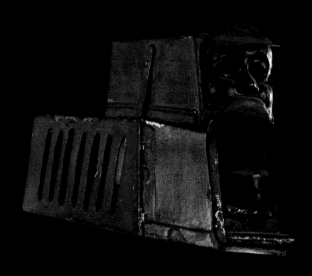

WAR AND (ETERNAL) PEACE

The terrible casualty lists of the Civil War tell us that the science of medicine was a long step behind the science of warfare in the last century. Alfred Stauch's 1860 "scarificator" for giving inoculations, which appears at the left, seems hopelessly primitive next to Henry Josselyn's remarkable twenty-shot revolver opposite, lower left, which was patented in 1866. August Rauh's pistol-sword from the same year held only six bullets but looks lethal enough. W. W. Marston's three-shot pistol opposite dates from 1857.

Once the weapons had done the
work, there were other cha
lenges to the inventor's ingenu
ity. John Reicherts' answer t
one of these appears below. H
patented his corpse preserve
which is designed to circulat
chilled air around the body, i
1868. Like most of the pater
models, it is done in miniature
the ice in the top is from our pho
tographer's refrigerator. It woul
be interesting to know more tha
we do about the memorial oppo
site. Why was it patent-worthy
Was it meant, in fact, to contai
the deceased friend? Alas, th
records have long since disap
peared, and we will never know

The patent models shown on page
49 are, clockwise from the top
a fruit dryer; a solar camera; a
sewing machine; a sleigh heater,
an animal tether; Charles Otis
first elevator; and a fluting iron.

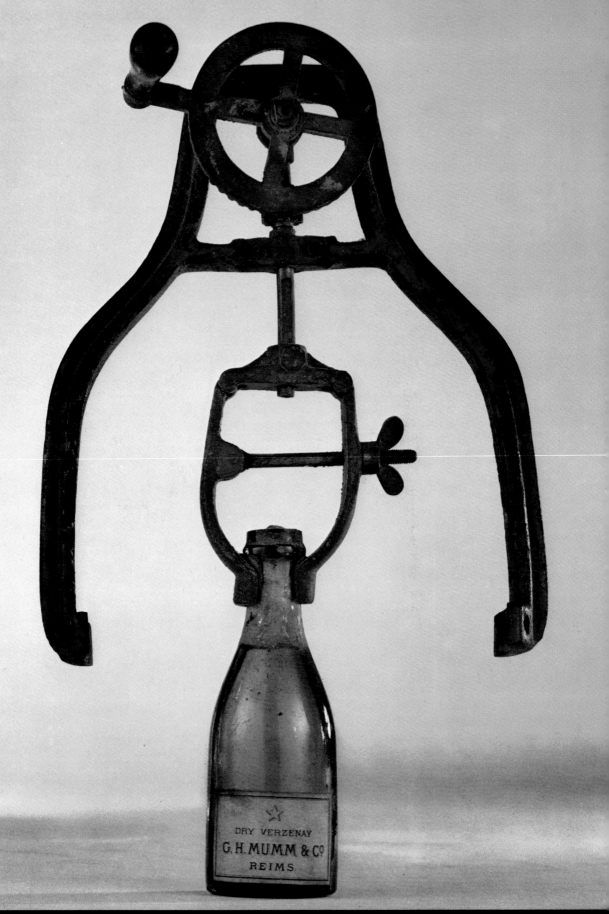

DRY VERZENAY

G. H. MUMM & C?

REIMS

ot every inventor was an Edison, of course, but few can have made quite so minute a contribution to mar

The lamplight filtering through the haze and drizzle gave the streets of New Orleans an eerie pallor that October night in 1890. It was nearing midnight when Dave Hennessy, the city's thirty-two-year-old police chief, left his office and headed home, escorted by an old friend, Captain William O'Connor. There had been threats on Hennessy's life, but the popular and respected chief took them lightly. When the two men reached Girod Street, where Hennessy lived, the chief told O'Connor it was not necessary to accompany him any farther. The two men bade each other good night, and Hennessy headed up the damp and deserted street alone.

He had almost reached home when the silence of the night was shattered by the roar of gunfire. The shots came from a shanty on the other side of the street where a recently arrived immigrant Sicilian shoemaker was living. Hennessy was hit, but he managed to draw his service revolver and get off three or four shots as his attackers fled.

Captain O'Connor heard the gunfire, rushed to the scene, and found Hennessy on Basin Street, where he had collapsed after gamely pursuing his assailants. "Who gave it to you, Dave?" O'Connor asked. "The Dagoes did it," Hennessy murmured.

Within hours the police found five weapons abandoned in the gutters a block or two from the scene of the crime. One was an ordinary double-barreled shotgun. The others were curious pieces—shotguns with the barrels sawed off and the stocks hinged so that the guns could be collapsed to the size of a horse pistol and easily concealed.

These weapons had done their work well. Three large slugs had torn vicious wounds in the chief. His face, neck, arms, and legs were riddled with shot. Hennessy lingered through the night in Charity Hospital but died the following morning.

VENDETTA IN NEW ORLEANS

The city panicked with fear of the Mafia when the police chief was murdered

Three victims of mob justice lie sprawled in the prison gallery where they were shot down.

Hennessy's body was taken back to the house on Girod Street where the bachelor chief had lived with his elderly mother, and later to City Hall, where it lay in state. The thousands that came to mourn him rivalled the crowds that had appeared there some months before to view the body of ex-Confederate President Jefferson Davis. The chief's brutal murder was on everybody's lips. Feeling against New Orleans' Italian community ran at fever pitch. One grief-stricken mourner, a news-carrier friend of the chief, went directly from the funeral to the Parish Prison, where he asked to see one of the arrested suspects, Antonio Scaffidi, and shot and wounded him in the neck.

The shots that killed David Hennessy in October were the belated echo of a salvo of gunfire that had split the New Orleans night five months before.

By JOSEPH E. PERSICO

The right to unload fruit vessels landing in New Orleans had been fiercely contested by two gangs of Italian stevedores, the Provenzanos and the Matrangas, so called after their rival bosses. Initially, the Provenzanos had controlled the business. But Charles Matranga, the operator of a gambling den and dance hall serving New Orleans blacks, began to eye the fruit-handling concession covetously when police pressure on his other enterprises became too uncomfortable. Through persuasion and coercion Matranga managed to oust the Provenzanos and put his own men on the wharves.

Late one night in May, seven of Matranga's men, including his brother Tony, were driving out Esplanade Street in a wagon after unloading a ship at the Levee. As the wagon reached a tree-lined intersection at Esplanade and Claiborne a fusillade of shotgun fire erupted, and three of the men fell wounded, including Tony Matranga, who lost a leg in the ambush.

At first the victims clung to the ancient Sicilian custom of silence and refused to identify their assailants. Later they relented and accused several members of the Provenzano faction. Six members of the Provenzano group were convicted in June.

The verdict left Chief Hennessy dissatisfied, and not merely because he was a personal friend of the Provenzanos. The attorneys for the Provenzano men had filed for a new trial, and in making an investigation relating to this appeal Hennessy had obtained damaging evidence of perjury by the witnesses for the Matrangas. Further feeding his suspicions that justice had been subverted was the fact that a key witness for the defense had been murdered before he could testify. Hennessy suspected the Matrangas of the deed. The Provenzano trial was, in fact, so redolent of perjury that the court did grant a new trial, set for October 22.

Hennessy's probing had convinced

him that the Matrangas were guilty of more than perjury and an isolated murder. In the course of his inquiries he had been in contact with Italian police officials and now had reason to believe that the Matranga faction represented the New Orleans branch of the Mafia.

Opinion differed as to whether the Mafia actually existed in America. However, ever since Italy had been united in 1861, her government had conducted a vigorous, often ruthless, crusade to stamp out the ancient criminal fraternity. In Sicily, Mafiosi were gunned down like dogs. Surely, some authorities believed, among the thousands of Italians then streaming to America there might be Mafiosi fleeing the harsh hand of the Italian police. In New Orleans, according to a grand-jury report, the Italian consulate had the names of over a thousand fugitives from Italian justice living among the city's twenty-five-thousand-member Italian colony. The city's total population was then about a quarter of a million.

The Sicilian criminal element had captured Hennessy's interest long before, and the young chief had carved out a national reputation as an authority on the Mafia. Nine years earlier Hennessy, then a detective, had scored an impressive coup by arresting the internationally notorious Sicilian bandit Giuseppe Esposito in New Orleans. This brigand was wanted in Italy for premeditated murder, robbery, and extortion. British authorities were after Esposito for mutilating a curate in a £5,000 ransom scheme.

But arresting a suspected Mafioso proved far simpler than getting a conviction. American police, trying to solve crimes believed committed by the Mafia, ran into the ancient Sicilian code of *omerta*, meaning, literally, "connivance." *Omerta* held that justice was a personal matter, not something to be delegated or entrusted

to outsiders. A man's first duty was to avenge himself for any injury. To appeal to the public, the police, or the courts for redress was contemptible, the act of a traitor. The customary Mafia penalty for giving evidence to the authorities was death.

Thanks to this near immunity from the testimony of their neighbors, blackmailers and extortionists exploited their fellow countrymen virtually at will in the New Orleans Italian colony. Authorities pointed despairingly to ninety-four murders involving Italians in the twenty-five years preceding the Hennessy assassination; only five had resulted in convictions, and the other cases had been dropped for lack of evidence.

The deadly feud between the Matrangas and Provenzanos hardened Hennessy's determination to break the Mafia in his city. He had obtained from Italian authorities criminal histories of several immigrants now residing in New Orleans. His investigations convinced him that Charles Matranga, Joseph P. Macheca, a well-to-do merchant, and several other Italian-Americans were the leaders of a Mafia family operating in the city. He had planned to destroy this criminal cabal by sending its leaders to prison for perjury in the first Provenzano trial.

In ferreting out the motive behind Hennessy's murder, the chief's fellow officers theorized that the Matranga leaders had been tipped off that Hennessy intended to put them behind bars. Hennessy was, in fact, murdered on October 15, exactly one week before he was expected to unveil his case against the Matranga gang at the second Provenzano trial.

Of those suspected as Mafia kingpins only Macheca was a native-born American. He gave every outward appearance of being a substantial and enterprising member of the community. Twenty years before, Joe Macheca had pioneered the steamship fruit trade between New Orleans and Central America. He owned the first ship to make the run and had founded the firm of Macheca Brothers. He was prominent in Democratic politics and often served as a delegate to the party's state conventions. Ironically, seventeen years earlier he had saved the life of a New Orleans police chief by his conspicuous heroism during a civil riot. Now middle-aged, Macheca was a portly, pleasant-mannered, and popular gentleman, father of six, owner of a handsome house on Bourbon Street, and believed to be worth hundreds of thousands of dollars. He was now a suspected architect of assassination.

The New Orleans populace was so enraged at the brazenness of the Hennessy killing that the mayor, Joseph A. Shakspeare, felt compelled to take extraordinary measures. Shakspeare described the murdered chief as a "victim of Sicilian vengeance" and warned, "We must teach these people a lesson that they will not forget for all time." The mayor appointed a committee of the city's prominent and powerful to help bring Hennessy's assassins to justice and to root out any "oath-bound" or "hell-born" societies in New Orleans. The appointees, who came to be known as the Committee of Fifty, put up a substantial sum of their own money to engage the best detective skills and the sharpest legal talent in the case.

After scores of initial arrests nineteen men were finally indicted on December 13, 1890, for the murder of David C. Hennessy. Later, the state obtained an order of severance, and only nine of the nineteen were scheduled for immediate trial. The nine were the alleged ringleaders, Joseph Macheca and Charles Matranga; Pietro Monasterio, the shoemaker living in the shanty from which the attack had been staged; Bastian Incardona, an Italian criminal fugitive; Antonio Marchesi, a fruit vendor; his fourteen-year-old son, Gaspare; Antonio Scaffidi and Antonio Bagnetto, also fruit vendors; and Emmanuele Polizzi, an unstable Sicilian who had

once been fired by the Provenzanos for blackmailing them.

The public's vengeful feeling against the Matranga-Macheca faction now seemed to work to the advantage of the rival Provenzanos. When the Provenzano members were finally retried in January, after postponement of the October trial date, they were found not guilty of the ambush on the Matrangas.

The date set for the Hennessy murder trial was February 16, 1891, with Judge Joshua G. Baker, a gentleman described as "pleasant, dignified and punctual," presiding. The

Slain police chief David C. Hennessy
Harper's Weekly, NOVEMBER 8, 1890

defense retained a blue-chip battery of five lawyers led by Thomas J. Semmes, one of the South's most distinguished attorneys, a former Louisiana attorney general and Confederate senator. The defense also boasted a former district attorney and crack trial lawyer, Lionel Adams. The high quality of counsel tended to confirm accounts that the defense was lavishly financed. The *New York Times* reported that Italians all over the country had been asked to contribute two dollars apiece to help defend their countrymen. Sums large and small flowing into New Orleans were estimated to have swelled the

defense war chest to seventy-five thousand dollars or more.

The Hennessy trial seemed to offer a clear-cut confrontation: a contest between a society based on law and a society rooted in evil, and the case commanded nationwide attention. The *New York Times* billed it in advance as "one of the noted criminal cases of the age." The selection of a jury foretold the intensity of the coming struggle. More than 1,300 prospective jurors had to be summoned, and 780 were examined. It took eleven days to select twelve jurymen.

On February 27 spectators packed the courtroom as the trial began. An uneasy stillness fell over the crowd as the first witness, Dr. Paul Archinard, assistant coroner, recounted the terrible wounds in Hennessy's body. Then the prosecution produced four witnesses who testified that "Peter Johnson," the man who had rented the shanty from which the shots were fired, was actually Joseph P. Macheca. The rent had been paid in advance by Macheca, who installed Monasterio in the shanty as a shoemaker shortly before the ambush.

A Mr. Peeler, a painter who lived on the corner near the murder scene, testified that on hearing the first shots he had sprung to his balcony and seen Scaffidi, Incardona, and Bagnetto firing from in front of Monasterio's shanty. He had seen Scaffidi fire twice at Hennessy with a double-barreled shotgun, reload, and fire again.

A black youth, Amos Scott, told the tense courtroom how Hennessy had been set up for the kill. Amos said he had talked to Gaspare Marchesi, the son of Antonio Marchesi, in Poydras Market three days after the shooting. Young Marchesi told Amos that on the fatal night he had been stationed by the men to watch for the police chief. When Hennessy appeared, Gaspare ran ahead of him and whistled to signal his approach.

Altogether the prosecution produced sixty-seven witnesses, including several who identified some of the accused as the men they had seen actually firing weapons or fleeing the murder scene.

In building its case the state had enjoyed unusual extralegal support, since the Committee of Fifty disclosed later that a spy had been planted as an employee of the defense team. This man was actually on the city's payroll, and his duty was to file a daily report of everything seen and heard in the defense camp.

The antics of one defendant, Emmanuele Polizzi, provided lively copy for the journalists covering the trial. Polizzi, a short, swarthy man in his late twenties who was described by a *Times* reporter as "dull and ignorant," had already interrupted the trial earlier with his ranting and had been taken into the judge's private chamber, where, it was rumored, he had offered a confession implicating the other defendants for an assurance of immunity for himself. On March 6, the day the defense was to begin presenting its case, Polizzi rushed to a window and shoved his foot through the glass in an attempt to escape to the street outside. Deputy sheriffs finally subdued him, but only after having their hands bitten and their clothes torn in a fierce struggle. Court was adjourned to give the coroner time to determine Polizzi's mental condition.

On March 7 the defense finally called its first witnesses, and the weight of evidence began to seesaw. Where the state's witnesses had Antonio Bagnetto firing at Hennessy, defense witnesses had him watching over some fruit stands in the marketplace during the attack. Others swore that the Marchesis, father and son, were at their home, four blocks away. Still other witnesses placed Scaffidi at home, nursing a sick wife, at the hour Hennessy was attacked.

Almost from the outset of the trial an undercurrent of insinuation and suspicion had swirled about the integrity of the jury. Gossip around the courthouse had it that "big money might be made by going on the jury and doing right." The money reportedly pouring into New Orleans to finance the defense tended to substantiate widespread suspicion of jury tampering. Toward the end of the trial two agents of D. C. O'Malley, a private detective working for the defense, actually were arrested and charged with attempting to bribe prospective jurors.

On Friday, the thirteenth of March, an impatient throng milled outside the courthouse. The jury had been out since the previous evening, and its verdict was due soon. At 2:53 P.M. the jury re-entered the courtroom, and the foreman handed the verdict to Judge Baker. The judge stared at it a full minute before ordering the verdict read. In the case of Macheca, Matranga, Bagnetto, Incardona, and the Marchesis the jury found "not guilty." In the case of Monasterio, Polizzi, and Scaffidi the jurors had not been able to agree on a verdict and had declared a mistrial.

As the *New York Times* reporter saw it, "So strong a case had been made by the State, the evidence had been so clear, direct and unchallenged, that the acquittal of the accused today came like a thunder clap from a clear sky." Among the crowd outside the courtroom disbelief soon gave way to outrage. The air was acrid with shouts and ominous mutterings. The frightened jurors prudently melted into the crowd.

But if, after the trial, the jurors worried about the public's attitude toward them, they expressed no misgivings about their judgment. A reporter questioned them shortly afterward. Some refused to comment, citing a pledge they had all made not to discuss the case further. But others, including the jury foreman, were willing to talk and expressed a low opinion of the prosecution's case. Why hadn't the prosecution called such obvious witnesses as Captain O'Connor and another police officer who had happened onto the murder scene? How reliable were eyewitnesses late on a rainy night in a dimly lit street? And hadn't the prosecution let the defense alibis go uncontradicted? One juror, acknowledging that the verdict may have "astonished" people, concluded, "If anybody could do any better than we did with the evidence, let them try."

The nine defendants could not be freed immediately after the trial, since technically they still faced another charge, "lying in wait with intent to commit murder." But in a day or two the state could be expected to drop this charge and set them free. Back in their cells the nine who had just been tried and the ten men still awaiting trial rejoiced in the verdict.

Along the Levee, people from the Italian colony began to gather in a festive mood. Italian boat owners in Lugger Bay near the French Market hoisted two flags on their masts—the Italian flag above, the Stars and Stripes below, upside down.

But as Italians celebrated on the Levee angry men met in another part of town to denounce the verdict and ponder other paths to justice. Several members of the Committee of Fifty had reconvened to form a "Vigilance Committee." That the Hennessy jury had been tampered with, the jurors bought off, and justice perverted was outrageously obvious to these men. Hadn't the defense somehow secured the list of prospective jurors even before the judge released it? Hadn't they been approached at home or on their way to the courthouse by defense emissaries with insinuations or outright offers of payment? Hadn't two of these bribers actually been arrested just before the trial ended? And what about the huge sums the defense had available to work its will?

Members of the Vigilance Committee labored until midnight drafting an appeal for a mass protest. It was signed by more than sixty prominent citizens. Their work done, the committee sent copies of the statement to the local newspapers.

Saturday, March 14, the morning after the trial, dawned cool, clear, and sunlit after a week of steady rain. Sheriff Gabriel Villère read in his newspaper the statement the Vigilance Committee had issued:

Mass Meeting

All good citizens are invited to attend a mass meeting on Saturday, March 14 at 10 o'clock A.M., at Clay Statue, to take steps to remedy the failure of justice in the Hennessy case. Come prepared for action.

If the call for action worried Sheriff Villère, he must have brushed his fears aside when he got to the Parish Prison and found nothing out of line. At 8:30 A.M. the sheriff left the prison in charge of his deputy, Captain Lem Davis, and headed for his office in City Hall.

Out on the Levee the city's Italians renewed the festivities of the night before and prepared for a victory banquet. A mile away, at the statue of Henry Clay, the sun was drawing a crowd certain to please the Vigilance Committee. Just before 10 A.M. W. S. Parkerson, a leader of the committee's call for action, a respected attorney and prominent politician, arrived on the scene. After leading a brief march around the base of the statue Parkerson mounted the pedestal and began to address the throng.

"What protection, or assurance of protection, is there left us," he cried, "when the very head of our police department—our chief of police—is assassinated, in our very midst, by the Mafia Society, and his assassins again turned loose on the community?... Will every man here follow me and see the murder of D. C. Hennessy vindicated? Are there men enough here to set aside the verdict of that infamous jury, every one of whom is a perjurer and a scoundrel?"

"Hang the murderers," the crowd shouted back.

By now the crowd had grown so great that the trolley cars circling Clay Statue could not move. Spectators clambered on top of the blocked cars and cheered the speaker on.

Two more speakers followed Parkerson, but the crowd was growing impatient. "We have had enough of words," men shouted, "now for action." The last speaker, a newspaper editor, John Wickliffe, was unable to finish. "Very well, then, gentlemen," he said, "let's go and do our duty. Mr. Parkerson is your leader. Mr. James D. Houston is your first lieutenant. Your second lieutenant is myself."

The leaders then walked over to Royal and Bienville streets, where about fifty men armed with pistols and shotguns joined them. The crowd, now swollen to well over six thousand and whipped to a righteous fury, began to march down Rampart Street toward the Parish Prison.

At the prison a swelling mass of onlookers now lined both sides of the street in front of the main gate. The Italian prisoners had learned of the mass meeting and begged Captain Davis to let them out, or else give them arms to defend themselves.

Davis was becoming edgy. Why wasn't his superior on the scene? He phoned Sheriff Villère to tell him of the surging crowd. He kept the night watch on duty when the day watch came to relieve them. He sent a runner out to bring in deputies who lived nearby. The crowd hooted and jeered as the prison gate clanged shut behind these reinforcements.

The prison that Davis was trying to secure was a bleak fortress occupying an entire city block. The main gate on Orleans Street was guarded by iron bars an inch and a half thick. But on Treme Street only a small wooden door gave entry into the prison. Davis ordered his carpenters to barricade this doorway. Each report of the carpenters' hammer blows was echoed by more yells from the crowd.

Matranga   *Macheca*

Monasterio   *Bagnetto*

The Marchesis, father and son

Scaffidi   *Polizzi*

MATRANGA: *The French Quarter* (KNOPF, 1936); BAGNETTO & SCAFFIDI: *Harper's Weekly*, NOV. 8, 1890; ALL OTHERS: CONTEMPORARY NEW ORLEANS *Times Democrat*, COURTESY NEW ORLEANS PUBLIC LIBRARY

Davis' strategy to save the nineteen prisoners was first to lock all the other inmates into their cells. He then transferred most of the Italians to the women's side of the prison, where they were released and allowed to fend for themselves within the prison compound. Several of the men bolted for hiding places—in a trash bin, in the wash house, under a mattress. Two even managed to cram themselves into an oversize doghouse that had been made out of an old box for Captain Davis' bull terrier, Queen. But most of the Italians remained upstairs on the women's side of the jail.

By now all four streets surrounding the prison were thick with people. Davis checked the carpenters' work on the Treme Street barricade and decided it would hold. Suddenly a new sound riveted the captain's attention. He could make out in the distance the muffled roar of an approaching mob, the steady tramp of marching feet. As he listened two detectives pulled up to the main gate in a horse-drawn cab and shouted to him that the Vigilance Committee was headed for the prison "to lynch the Dagoes." Davis answered, "Let them come, they won't get in."

Pasquale Corte, the Italian consul in New Orleans, had also read the Vigilance Committee's call to action that morning in the papers. To Corte this threat was a direct summons to duty. At least three of the men accused of the crime were still Italian citizens and entitled to the Italian government's protection.

When Corte learned that a crowd was indeed gathering at Clay Statue, he raced his carriage to City Hall to find Mayor Shakspeare. There he met Sheriff Villère and the attorney general, Mr. Rogers, who told the consul that they too were looking for the mayor. But in Corte's judgment, "They appeared to me to be very calm and to be anticipating what was about to happen."

Corte, a tough and determined agent of his government, then asked where he might find Governor Francis Nicholls. Told to try a certain lawyer's office, Corte hurried back to the carriage and tracked Nicholls down. The Italian diplomat pleaded with the Louisiana governor to send troops or a force of police to head off possible violence at the prison. Nicholls replied that he could do nothing until he received a request from the mayor; that he had already telephoned Mayor Shakspeare at the Pickwick Club and asked him to

Illustrated American, APRIL 4, 1891

Vigilante leader William S. Parkerson

come over at once. Nicholls suggested that Corte sit down and wait with him. Twenty-five agonizing minutes passed; then the telephone finally rang, and someone reported that the mob had reached the prison. Corte sprang to his carriage and headed at full speed to reach the scene of the trouble.

The mob arrived at the Parish Prison and demanded the keys from Captain Davis. He refused. The iron-barred main gate looked formidable, but the barricaded wooden door on Treme Street offered the vigilantes a more vulnerable target. A pile of wood on the street provided handy battering-rams. Neighbors volunteered their axes for the task. A black man brought a heavy stone crashing down on the door. It burst open, and a roar went up from the crowd.

John Wickliffe stood guard at the shattered entrance and allowed sixty armed men to enter. The merely curious were excluded. Sentries were posted at every exit to shoot down any prisoner trying to escape.

Parkerson helped to lead a group of vigilantes, rifles slung over their shoulders, across the prison yard. The guards quickly backed out of harm's way. As the vigilantes entered the prison building they saw in one cell a face frozen in terror. It was Scaffidi, somebody said. Shots rang out and the man dropped, though they had missed him. He was not one of the nineteen Italians. The leaders asked for someone to come forward who could identify the right prisoners. Somebody shouted, "Go to the female department." The door to the women's section was thrown open, and an old black woman told the vigilantes they would find the men they wanted upstairs.

The avengers first discovered young Gaspare Marchesi but spared the boy because of his youth. His father, Antonio, had fled with Scaffidi and Macheca to the gallery for condemned prisoners on the third floor. A grated gate slammed and locked behind them. The gate at the other end of the corridor was locked too, trapping the three men like caged beasts. They tried to protect themselves by lining up behind a pillar in the gallery. The mob reached the third floor, but the locked gate kept them from getting directly at the prisoners. Scaffidi peered out briefly, and he was shot through the head. Marchesi stumbled over Scaffidi's fallen body and, while struggling to his feet, was riddled with buckshot. Someone unlocked the gate for the vigilantes. They moved in and made short work of Joseph Macheca. He slumped to the floor, and the avengers passed over him.

Six other prisoners had fled down a back stairway and hidden in a cell until discovered by half a dozen gunmen. They then burst into the courtyard, where they were finally trapped against a wall. The six huddled piteously on their knees, their hands over their heads, pleading for mercy. The executioners poured a deadly rain of fire into the crouching figures, who fell in a blood-soaked heap. Monasterio, still alive, raised a hand. "Give him another load," someone shouted. A revolver shot dispatched the shoemaker for good.

To satisfy the crowd, which had missed the action within the prison, Antonio Bagnetto was dragged outside and hanged from a tree, although the man was probably dead already from gunshot wounds.

The crazed Polizzi was found crouched under a staircase, babbling to himself. He too was dragged before the mob. A rope was thrown around his neck, and he was hoisted to a lamppost. Polizzi managed to grab the rope and pull himself up, hand over hand, until he reached the crossbar and hung there gasping. A young man climbed the post and beat him in the face until the prisoner lost his grip and fell to the ground. Finally, on the fourth attempt, with his hands tied behind him, Polizzi was hanged. The crowd gave out a deafening cheer.

One of those who arrived too late to witness the spectacle, or to help avert it, was Pasquale Corte. On reaching the jail the Italian consul realized the massacre was over and headed back to his office, where he would soon be occupied in the grim business of helping the families of the victims.

Twenty minutes after the Treme Street door had burst open, it was over. Eleven men lay dead. The other

Cornered in the courtyard by the angry avengers, six prisoners begged for mercy—in vain.

eight Italian prisoners were spared, either because they had not been found or someone had vouched for their innocence. For those who still had not seen enough, arrangements were made for small groups of ten to fifteen spectators each to pass through the prison to witness the vigilantes' handiwork.

Mr. Parkerson addressed the crowd once more: "I called you together for a duty. You have performed that duty. Now, go home and God bless you."

"God bless you, Mr. Parkerson," they shouted back, lifting him to their

shoulders for a triumphal return to Clay Statue.

Among the original nine defendants who survived were Bastian Incardona and Charles Matranga. Incardona had hidden in a box of rubbish. Matranga, one of the suspected ringleaders, had taken refuge under a mattress, a crucifix pressed to his lips. His deliverance, he later told reporters, had confirmed his innocence. He expressed some doubts, however, about the innocence of the less fortunate prisoners.

As the *New Delta*, the city's leading Democratic daily, later described that March morning, "The work was rapid and comprehensive. The guilty were stricken, the innocent were spared." Perhaps so. But of the eleven dead men now stretched out in the prison, three had been acquitted, the jury could not agree on a verdict for three others, and five had never been tried at all.

When word of the lynching reached Lugger Landing, flags were quickly lowered, some to half-mast. By Sunday the only Italian flag still flying was one from the masthead of a steamship of the Macheca line. That Sunday afternoon the founder of the firm was carried from his Bourbon Street house in an expensive silver- and gold-trimmed casket. Twenty-five carriages bearing Joseph P. Macheca's relatives, friends, and associates followed the hearse to the funeral in St. Louis Cathedral and then to the cemetery.

The funerals of the other victims were less splendid. Most were simple family observances. Bagnetto's body was attended by no one. Three of the men were buried in potter's field.

The gunfire in the Parish Prison reverberated around the country and beyond. Italian-Americans meeting in Chicago fired off a telegram to Secretary of State James G. Blaine: "We, Italians by birth, Americans by choice, assembled in mass meeting, unanimously protest against the cowardly and lawless act of the New Orleans mob, aided by the tacit consent of the local authorities. . . ." In New York six thousand members of the Italian community massed at Cooper Union in an orderly but angry demonstration. Outraged Italians gathered in Pittsburgh, Philadelphia, and Kansas City.

In Italy Premier Antonio Starabba di Rudini now faced a threat to his political survival. In office only one month, possessing only the slenderest parliamentary majority, Rudini was already in trouble on a tax-reduction pledge when the New Orleans incident broke. Since some of the vic-

tims were still Italian citizens, public opinion clamored for justice and the vindication of Italy's national honor.

Rudini took a time-honored stance, a show of strength abroad to mask his faltering grip at home. He demanded punishment of the murderers and indemnity for the families of the victims. In a lengthy exchange of diplomatic notes Secretary Blaine lectured the Italians on the fine points of American federalism, under which Washington could make no such assurances in a matter essentially involving the state of Louisiana. Naturally, this answer could not satisfy the embattled Rudini. He ordered Baron Fava, the Italian ambassador, home from Washington in order to register Italy's official displeasure.

Rumors now began to spread of Italian warships headed for the American coast. The threat, however fanciful, was just the tonic the American spirit thirsted for in 1891. The war scare, fanned by a jingoistic press, gave Americans a chance to demonstrate, after a quarter of a century, that the deep wounds of the Civil War were healing nicely and that the nation was, once again, whole. Confederate veterans from Tennessee and the Shelby Rifles of Texas volunteered to fight for Old Glory against Rome. Uniontown, Alabama, offered fifteen hundred men. An ex-Confederate wrote the Secretary of War, ". . . I will . . . fight for the old flag as willingly as I fought against [it]." From Georgia the War Department received an offer of "a company of unterrified Georgia rebels to invade Rome, disperse the Mafia and plant the Stars and Stripes on the dome of St. Peter's." Not until the Spanish-American War would America have a better chance to satisfy the country's longing for a true test of renewed national unity.

On May 5 a New Orleans grand jury, convened to look into the Parish

Prison murders, issued its report. As for the trial, the grand jury concluded that some of the jurors who had served on the Hennessy jury had been subject to "a money influence to control their decision." As a result six men were indicted for attempted bribery, including the private detective, D. C. O'Malley. Only one person was actually convicted, and he received a short sentence.

As for the lynch mob, the grand jury decided that it "embraced several thousand of the first, best and even the most law-abiding citizens of the city . . . in fact, the act seemed to involve the entire people of the parish and the City of New Orleans. . . ." And after thoroughly examining the subject the grand jury reported there was no reason to indict anybody for the lynching.

Not everyone who studied the case shared this judgment. During the diplomatic sparring between the United States and Italy, the Department of Justice had been ordered to look into the incident. After reviewing the eight-hundred-page transcript of the Hennessy trial, a U.S. attorney, William Grant, reported that the evidence against the defendants was "exceedingly unsatisfactory" and inconclusive. And later, all charges outstanding against those who had survived the prison massacre were dropped.

No matter. The mass of public sentiment across the nation leaned to the view that justice had triumphed—in the streets of New Orleans, if not in its courts. A scattering of civil libertarians might shake their heads sadly. The *Nation* magazine did say we had "cut a sorry figure before the civilized world." But New Orleans was content. "The hand of the assassin has been stayed," the *New Delta* reported. "The Mafia is a thing of the past."

Joseph E. Persico, a special assistant to Governor Nelson Rockefeller of New York, serves as the governor's chief speech writer.

no dearth of students, but qualified students, especially females, were another matter. Few girls could have proceeded directly from knitting nightcaps in a dame school to "calculation of and projection of the eclipses of the luminaries." At least one enterprising Pennsylvania teacher seems to have recognized the problem. He advertised that the rules of arithmetic would be "peculiarly adapted to the (female) sex, so as to render them concise and familiar." A flourishing textbook industry quickly developed to serve the needs of lady scholars. A few of the more popular titles seem to indicate that girls were not always seizing their chance to learn navigation, gauging, and spherical trig. In great demand, however, were *The Matrimonial Preceptor; The Compleat Housewife or Accomplish'd Gentlewoman;* and *The Ladies' Friend, being a treatise on the virtues and qualifications . . . of the fair sex, so as to render them most agreeable to the sensible part of mankind . . . to which is annexed, Real Beauty; or the Art of Charming, by an ingenious Poet.* All of these appeared during the 1760's and enjoyed very respectable sales.

Such books promised to supplement class work by spelling out "a Girl's duty to God and her Parents," instruction on how to make "the choice of a Husband," and almost always included recipes and household hints. *The Matrimonial Preceptor* not only gave advice to spinsters and matrons on the capture, care, and feeding of a husband, but it also contained "a Thousand other Points, Essential to Husbands." The section designed to be read by husbands emphasized patience, understanding, and tolerance. The several "elegant" authors of this anthology of essays rather surprisingly included Mr. Samuel Richardson, better known for *Clarissa,* and Mr. Henry Fielding, famous for *Tom Jones,* as well as Alex-

ander Pope, Ovid, and a mixed bag of other illustrious belle-lettrists. The publication notice promised a "Collection of Most Excellent Examples Relating to the Married State," among which were *The Folly of precipitate Matches, The Brutality of Husbands,* and *The Duties of a good Wife.* The witty and satirical tone of Richardson's, Fielding's, and Pope's other works is largely missing in *The Matrimonial Preceptor,* and Ovid has been drastically edited. As with the rules of arithmetic, peculiar adaptations seem to have been indicated.

Emma Willard

Many of the adventure schools hedged their financial risks by functioning as a combination store and educational institution, selling fancywork, "very good Orange-Oyl," sweetmeats, sewing notions, painted china, and candles along with lessons in dancing, foreign languages, geography, penmanship, and spelling. Usually they were mama-and-papa affairs, with the wife instructing girls in "curious works" and the husband concentrating upon "higher studies." Curious works covered a great

deal of ground—the making of artificial fruits and flowers, the "raising of paste," enamelling, japanning, quilting, fancy embroidery, and in at least one recorded case "flowering on catgut," an intriguing accomplishment that has passed into total oblivion, leaving no surviving examples.

The adventure schools advertised heavily in newspapers and journals of the period, often in terms indicating that teaching was not an especially prestigious profession. One Thomas Carroll took several columns in a May, 1765, issue of the New York *Mercury* to announce a curriculum that would have taxed the entire faculty of Harvard and then proceeded to explain that he "was not under the necessity of coming here to teach, he had views of living more happy, but some unforeseen and unexpected events have happened since his arrival here . . . ," thus reducing this Renaissance paragon to schoolkeeping and his lady to teaching French knots and quilting.

While they lasted adventure schools attempted to offer something for everyone, including adults, and came in all forms, sizes, and price ranges. They met anywhere and everywhere: "at the Back of Mr. Benson's Brew-House," in rented halls, in borrowed parlors, at inns, and from time to time in barns or open fields. The adventurer was usually available for private lessons as well, making house calls "with the utmost discretion," especially in the case of questionable studies like dancing or French verbs. The entire physical plant usually fitted easily into a carpetbag. In comparison to the pittance paid to the keepers of dame schools the tuition charged by these teachers must have seemed astronomically high—a shilling an hour for language classes and whatever the traffic would stand for the more recondite specialties. Fees were negotiable, and the socially prominent often received favorable rates in the hope that they would lend cachet and attract a wider clientele.

The pretentious and empty promises of the adventure schools eventually aroused considerable criticism. Americans may not yet have appreciated the value of female education, but they seem always to have known the value of a dollar. It was not long before the public realized that flowering on catgut was not so useful an accomplishment for their daughters as ciphering or reading. The more marginal operators began to melt away, and those schoolmasters who hung on were obliged to devote more attention to practical subjects and eliminate many of the patent absurdities.

Penmanship classes, often separate enterprises, flourished everywhere from the 1750's on, and one John Wingfield of New York promised to teach the art within three months for a flat fee of five dollars. Wingfield's ads were grimly pragmatic, stressing the importance of a fine hand for those who could so easily fall into the "Melancholy State of Widowhood." "For want of this [skill]," ran Wingfield's notice in the New York *Gazette,* "how often do we see women, when they are left to shift for themselves [in the M.S.O.W.], obliged to leave their Business to the Management of others; sometimes to their great Loss, and Sometimes to their utter Ruin." "Business," "Loss," and "Ruin" seem to have been the operative words, and the penmanship schools were thronged. As a testament to their newly acquired proficiency graduates were awarded diplomas decorated by fancifully penned flora and fauna, suitable for framing. Swans, which lent themselves easily to Spencerian flourishes and curves, seem to have been a particular favorite. The study of arithmetic was also urged for similar reasons, as were reading and grammar. It quickly became obvious that literacy could increase earning power —or at least *saving* power—and

while America was still a very long way from accepting the notion that a woman might *choose* to support herself, people did acknowledge that there were some cases when she might have no option.

Certain religious groups, particularly the Moravians and the Quakers, had always eschewed frippery and pioneered in the more realistic education of women. Friends' schools were organized as soon as the size and prosperity of the settlements permitted them. This training emphasized housewifery but did include the fundamentals of literacy. Many of the earliest eighteenth-century Quaker primary schools were co-educational, though access to them was limited to the immediate community. Because these were concentrated in the Philadelphia area, girls born in Pennsylvania had a much better chance of acquiring some education than their contemporaries elsewhere. The Moravians (who also settled in the southeastern states) quickly recognized the general lack of facilities in the rest of the Colonies and offered boarding arrangements in a few of their schools. The student body soon included intrepid and homesick girls from New England and even the West Indies. These institutions were purposeful and rather solemn, the antithesis of superficiality. The Moravians insisted upon communal household chores as well as domestic skills, and in the eighteenth century these obligations could be onerous; dusting, sweeping, spinning, carding, and weaving came before embroidery and hemstitching. These homely lessons were enlivened by rhymes celebrating the pleasure of honest work. Examples survive in the seminary archives and supply a hint of the uplifting atmosphere:

I've spun seven cuts, dear companions allow
That I am yet little, and know not right how;

Mine twenty and four, which I finished with joy,
And my hands and my feet did willing employ.

Though the teaching sisters in these

sectarian schools seem to have been kind and patient, the life was rigorous and strictly ordered, a distinct and not always popular alternative to pleasant afternoons with easygoing adventure masters. In an era when education for women was still widely regarded as a luxury for the upper classes, the appeal of the pioneering religious seminaries tended to be somewhat narrow. If a family happened to be sufficiently well-off to think of educating their girls, the tendency was to make fine ladies of them. As a result there were many young women who could carry a tune but not a number, who could model a passable wax apple but couldn't read a recipe, who had memorized the language of flowers but had only the vaguest grasp of English grammar. There seemed to be no middle ground between the austerities of the religious schools and the hollow frivolities offered by commercial ventures. Alternatives did not really exist until the 1820's, when the earliest tentative attempts were made to found independent academies and seminaries.

Catherine and Harriet Beecher, who were among the first to open a school designed to bridge this gulf, believed almost as strongly as the Moravians in the importance of domestic economy. They were, however, obliged by public demand to include a long list of dainty accomplishments in their Hartford curriculum. Many girls continued to regard the new secular seminaries as they had the adventure schools—as rival shops where they could browse or buy at will, dropping in and out at any time they chose. To the despair of the well-intentioned founders few students ever stayed to complete the course at any one place. Parents judged a school as if it were a buffet table, evaluating it by the number and variety of subjects displayed. In writing later of the difficult beginnings of the Hartford Seminary, Catherine Beecher said that "all was

When "woman's sphere" expanded to include teaching, the education of girls in America became more realistic. Certainly this daguerreotype, made around 1850, of a class in a Boston school seems to portray serious study seriously pursued.

perpetual haste, imperfection, irregularity, and the merely mechanical commitment of words to memory, without any chance for imparting clear and connected ideas in a single branch of knowledge. The review of those days is like the memory of a troubled and distracting dream."

Public opinion about the education of girls continued to be sharply (if never clearly) divided until after the Civil War. Those who pioneered in the field were at the mercy of socially ambitious and ambivalent parents, confused and unevenly prepared students, and constantly shifting social attitudes. In sudden and disconcerting switches the "friends" of women's education often turned out to be less than wholehearted in their advocacy. Benjamin Rush, whose *Thoughts Upon Female Education,* written in 1787, influenced and inspired Emma Willard, Mary Lyon, and the Beecher sisters, later admitted that his thoughtful considerations had finally left him "not enthusiastical upon the subject." Even at his best, Rush sounds no more than tepid; American ladies, he wrote, "should be qualified to a certain degree by a peculiar and suitable education to concur in instructing their sons in the principles of liberty and government." During her long editorship of *Godey's Lady's Book* Sarah Josepha Hale welcomed every new female seminary and academy but faithfully reminded her readers that the sanctity of the home came first: ". . . on what does social well-being rest but in our homes . . . ?" "Oh, spare our homes!" was a constant refrain, this chorus coming from the September, 1856, issue. *Godey's Lady's Book* reflects the pervasive nineteenth-century fear that the educated woman might be a threat to the established and symbiotic pattern of American family life. The totally ignorant woman, on the other hand, was something of an embarrassment to the new nation. The country was inundated by visiting European jour-

nalists during this period, and they invariably commented upon the dullness of our social life and the disappointing vacuity of the sweet-faced girls and handsome matrons they met. Though Americans themselves seemed to feel safer with a bore than with a bluestocking, they were forced to give the matter some worried thought.

"If all our girls become philosophers," the critics asked, "who will darn our stockings and cook the meals?" It was widely, if somewhat irrationally, assumed that a maiden who had learned continental stitch-

Mary Lyon, founder of Mount Holyoke

ery upon fine lawn might heave to and sew up a shirt if necessary, but few men believed that a woman who had once tasted the heady delights of Shakespeare's plays would ever have dinner ready on time—or at all.

The founders of female seminaries were obliged to cater to this unease by modifying their plans and their pronouncements accordingly. The solid academic subjects were so generally thought irrelevant for "house-

wives and helpmeets" that it was usually necessary to disguise them as something more palatable. The Beechers taught their girls chemistry at Hartford but were careful to assure parents and prospective husbands that its principles were applicable in the kitchen. The study of mathematics could be justified by its usefulness in running a household. Eventually the educators grew more daring, recommending geology as a means toward understanding the Deluge and other Biblical mysteries and suggesting geography and even history as suitable because these studies would "enlarge women's sphere of thought, rendering them more interesting as companions to men of science." There is, however, little evidence that many were converted to this extreme point of view. The average nineteenth-century American man was not at all keen on chat with an interesting companion, preferring a wife like the one in the popular jingle "*who never learnt the art of schooling/Untainted with the itch of ruling.*" The cliché of the period was "woman's sphere." The phrase was so frequently repeated that it acquires almost physical qualities. Woman's Sphere—the nineteenth-century woman was fixed and sealed within it like a model ship inside a bottle. To tamper with the arrangement was to risk ruining a complex and fragile structure that had been painstakingly assembled over the course of two centuries. Just one ill-considered jolt might make matchwood of the entire apparatus.

In 1812 the anonymous author of *Sketches of the History, Genius, and Disposition of the Fair Sex* wrote that women are "born for a life of uniformity and dependence. . . . Were it in your power to give them genius, it would be almost always a useless and very often a dangerous present. It would, in general, make them regret the station which Providence has assigned them, or have recourse to unjustifiable ways to get from it." The writer identified himself only as a "friend of the sex" (not actually specifying which one).

This century's feminists may rage at and revel in such quotes, but the nineteenth-century educators were forced to live with this attitude and work within and around it. In order to gain any public or private support for women's secondary schools they had to prove that a woman would not desert her husband and children as soon as she could write a legible sentence or recite a theorem. That fear was genuine, and the old arguments resurfaced again and again. What about Saint Paul's injunction? What about the sanctity of the home? What about the health of the future mothers of the race? What about supper?

Advocates of secondary education for women, therefore, became consummate politicians, theologians, hygienists, and, when necessary, apologists. "It is desirable," wrote Mary Lyon in 1834 of her Mount Holyoke Female Seminary project, "that the plans relating to the subject should not seem to originate with us but with benevolent *gentlemen*. If the object should excite attention there is danger that many good men will fear the effect on society of so much female influence and what they will call female greatness." New and subtle counterarguments were presented with great delicacy. God had entrusted the tender minds of children to women; therefore women were morally obliged to teach. The home would be a holier place if the chatelaine understood religious principles and could explain them. The founders of Abbot Academy proclaimed that "to form the immortal mind to habits suited to an immortal being, and to instill principles of conduct and form the character for an immortal destiny, shall be subordinate to no other care." All that harping on immortality went down smoothly in the evangelistic atmosphere of the 1820's. A thick coating of religion was applied to every

new educational venture. The parents of prospective students were assured that their daughters would not only study religion in class but would have twice-daily periods of silent meditation, frequent revival meetings, compulsory chapel services, and a Sunday that included all of these. In reading the early seminary catalogues, one finds it hard to see where secular studies could have fit in at all. To the religious guarantees were appended promises of careful attention to health. The educators lost no time in adding the new science of calisthenics to their curricula.

By 1893 Mount Holyoke could teach zoology without pretending it was domestic science.

They had the medical records of their students compared to that of the public at large and published the gratifying results in newspapers and magazines. Domestic work was also to be required of girls who attended the new seminaries, partly for economy's sake but mainly so that they would not forget their ultimate destiny.

All of this was calming and persuasive, but nothing was so effective

as simple economics. By the 1830's most states had begun a program of primary public education. As the West followed suit the need for teachers became acute and desperate. Men were not attracted to the profession because the pay was wretched, the living conditions were lonely, and the status of a schoolmaster was negligible if not downright laughable. Saint Paul was revised, updated, and finally reversed. He had not, after all, envisioned the one-room schoolhouses of the American prairie, the wages of three dollars a month, or the practice of "boarding

around."

Within an astonishingly short time fears for female health subsided. The first women teachers proved amazingly durable, able to withstand every rigor of frontier life. In a letter to her former headmistress one alumna of the Hartford Seminary described accommodations out west:

I board where there are eight children,

and the parents, and only two rooms in the house. I must do as the family do about washing, as there is but one basin, and no place to go to wash but out the door. I have not enjoyed the luxury of either lamp or candle, their only light being a cup of grease with a rag for a wick. Evening is my only time to write, but this kind of light makes such a disagreeable smoke and smell, I cannot bear it, and do without light, except the fire. I occupy a room with three of the children and a niece who boards here. The other room serves as a kitchen, parlor, and bedroom for the rest of the family. . . .

Other graduates were just as stoical and often no more comfortable:

I board with a physician, and the house has only two rooms. One serves as kitchen, eating, and sitting room; the other, where I lodge, serves also as the doctor's office, and there is no time, night or day, when I am not liable to interruption.

My school embraces both sexes, and all ages from five to seventeen, and not one can read intelligibly. They have no idea of the proprieties of the schoolroom or of study. . . . My furniture consists now of . . . benches, a single board put up against the side of the room for a writing desk, a few bricks for andirons, and a stick of wood for shovel and tongs.

These letters were collected by Catherine Beecher in her book *True Remedy for the Wrongs of Women*, which advanced the cause of women's education by showing the worthwhile uses to which it could be put. Delighted with the early results, several states quickly set up committees to consider training women teachers on a larger scale. Their findings were favorable, though couched in oddly ambiguous language. New York's group reported that women seemed to be "endued with peculiar faculties" for the occupation. "While man's nature is rough, stern, impatient, ambitious, hers is gentle, tender, enduring, unaspiring." That was most encouraging, but the gentlemen also generously acknowledged that "the habits of female teachers are better and their morals purer; they are much more apt to be content with, and continue in, the occupation of teaching." A Michigan report stated in 1842 that "an elementary school, where the rudiments of an English education only are taught, such as reading, spelling, writing, and the outlines barely of geography, arithmetic, and grammar, requires a female of practical common sense with amiable and winning manners, a patient spirit, and a tolerable knowledge of the springs of human action. A female thus qualified, carrying with her into the schoolroom the gentle influences of her sex, will do more to inculcate right morals and prepare the youthful intellect for the severer discipline of its after years, than the most accomplished and learned male teacher." Far from objecting to these rather condescending statements, the founders of the struggling seminaries were more than happy to hear them. Even the miserable wages offered to teachers could be regarded as an advantage, since they provided the single most effective argument for more female academies. "But where are we to raise such an army of teachers as are required for this great work?"

Elaine Kendall learned about the educational plight of females in early America while doing background research for a book on women's colleges. Her book, to be called Peculiar Institutions, *will be published next year by G. P. Putnam's Sons.*

asked Catherine Beecher in the same book that contained the letters from her ex-students. "Not from the sex which finds it so much more honorable, easy, and lucrative, to enter the many roads to wealth and honor open in this land. . . . It is WOMAN who is to come [forth] at this emergency, and meet the demand— woman, whom experience and testimony have shown to be the best, as well as the cheapest guardian and teacher of childhood, in the school as well as the nursery."

Teaching became a woman's profession by default and by rationalization. Clergymen and theologians suddenly had nothing but praise for women teachers. God must have meant them to teach because he made them so good at it. They would work for a half or a third of the salary demanded by a man. What, after all, was a schoolroom but an extension of the home, woman's natural sphere? And if females had to have schools of their own to prepare them for this holy mission, then so be it. Future American generations must not be allowed to suffer for want of instruction when a Troy, Hartford, or Mount Holyoke girl asked no more than three dollars a month, safe escort to the boondocks, and a candle of her own. ☆

MAN FLY?

MR. JEFFERSON

HEDGES

Thomas Jefferson had just turned seventy-nine when he was asked his opinion, by a Mr. D. B. Lee, on man's being able to devise a means of flying. Here is his reply:

Monticello April 27–22

Sir
your letter of the 15th is received, but Age has long since obliged me to withold my mind from Speculations of the difficulty of those of your letter, that their are means of artifical buoyancy by which man may be supported in the Air, the Balloon has proved, and that means of dirrecting it may be discovered is against no law of Nature and is therefore possible as in the case of Birds, but to do this by macanacal means alone in a medium so rare and unresisting as air must have the aid of some principal not yet generaly known. however I can realy give no oppinion understandingly on the subject and with more good will than Confidence wish you Success
Th Jefferson

T.R.'s Last Adventure CONTINUED FROM PAGE 38

younger Roosevelt would go ahead in a light canoe with a sighting rod; finding a point with a good vista upstream and down, he would land and set up the rod. Upstream, Lyra would estimate the distance as Rondon took directions with a compass and recorded the figures. While they moved on to where Kermit had been standing he would continue downstream to establish a new point. During that first half-day Kermit landed nearly a hundred times, and the surveyors made but nine and a third kilometers.

T.R. ran ahead in his canoe, through "a lofty and matted forest [that] rose like a green wall on either hand." The trees were "stately and beautiful. . . . looped and twisted vines hung from them like great ropes." Fragrant scents blew from flowers on the banks, and apart from an occasional bird call out of the depths of the forest, all was silent. The Colonel only travelled a few hours on February 27, then pulled ashore to make camp and wait for the surveyors. It had rained at intervals during the day—this was toward the end of the rainy season—but after sunset the sky cleared. "The stars were brilliant overhead," Roosevelt wrote, "and the new moon hung in the west. It was a pleasant night, the air almost cool, and we slept soundly." The following morning T.R. stayed on in camp after the surveyors started downstream to wait for Cherrie, who was gathering specimens in the nearby forests. It was almost noon before the two embarked again on the Dúvida's "swirling brown current." It seemed as if it was going to be a leisurely and relaxing journey for Roosevelt.

The second day on the river the party registered an advance of sixteen and a half kilometers, and the third day—in rain that went from showers

to "vertical sheets of water"—they travelled and recorded twenty and a half kilometers. For the first time they detected signs of Indian habitation: abandoned palm-leaf shelters, overgrown planting fields, the vine handrail of a washed-away pole bridge. Cherrie shot a large monkey, which proved "very good eating." Sunday, March 2, their fourth day, was again almost without rain, and

White water ahead often signalled the approach of still another stretch of rapids.
KERMIT ROOSEVELT; LIBRARY OF CONGRESS

T.R. found it "delightful to drift and paddle slowly down the beautiful tropical river." The current was slow, and "the broad, deep, placid stream bent and curved in every direction, although the general course was northwest." The country through which they were travelling was flat, noted the Colonel, "and more of the land was under than above water. Continually we found ourselves travelling between stretches of marshy forest where for miles the water stood or ran among the trees." In midafternoon

the current quickened, became faster and faster "until it began to run like a mill-race, and we heard the roar of rapids ahead." The dugouts were pulled ashore so that a survey could be made.

Stretching for nearly a mile, with many curls and several drops of at least six feet, the rapids proved to be a serious obstacle. At one point the river narrowed to less than two yards between ledges of naked rock. "It seemed extraordinary, almost impossible," the Colonel marvelled, "that so broad a river could in so short a space of time contract its dimensions to the width of the strangled channel through which it now poured its entire volume." Kneeling at the narrowest point and leaning out over the water, Cherrie found that he could touch the opposite shore with the muzzle of his rifle. No canoe could get through the channel's whirlpools. It took the expedition two and a half days to make a portage of these first rapids. They camped above the rapids on March 2, the next day moved their baggage to the foot of the rapids, and on March 4 and the morning of the fifth dragged the dugouts across a road chopped through the forests. The heavy, cumbersome boats were moved with the aid of several hundred small logs cut to serve as rollers and placed about two yards apart. Two men harnessed to a dragrope pulled, while a third pried with a lever behind; and thus each canoe, "bumping and sliding, was twitched through the woods."

Not only did the portage cost the party two and half days of "severe and incessant labor"; it also resulted in some damage to the dugouts. When the canoes were launched again below the rapids, one of the boats filled with water and went to the bottom, and more hard work was needed to raise it. For the first time, perhaps, the vastness of their undertaking struck the members of the expedition. Gathered around the campfire after dinner, the men discussed what might lie ahead. They realized that they did not know whether they had one hundred or eight hundred kilometers to go; whether the stream would continue smooth and calm or be broken by innumerable rapids, such as the ones just encountered; whether hostile Indians lurked in the surrounding darkness. "We had no idea how much time the trip would take," Roosevelt reflected. "We had entered a land of unknown possibilities."

On March 5 the explorers made twelve kilometers, and by three o'clock the following day they had made nineteen. In the lead, T.R. once more noted the quickening of the current that indicated rapids ahead and signalled the party ashore. It took three days to make a second portage, and on a foraging journey downstream Kermit discovered a third set of rapids only five or six kilometers below the second. On the tenth they unloaded the canoes a third time, carried the burdens down, and lowered the boats through the swirling waters of the lesser rapids. Even though it was dangerous to work nearly naked in the river and they were constantly plagued by biting and stinging insects, this was preferable to manhandling the dugouts overland. T.R. found that termites had eaten holes in his sun helmet and in the cover of his cot. During the night the two older canoes filled with water in the rising river, sank, and were broken apart on boulders along the river bottom. Wryly naming the place Broken Canoe Rapids, the expedition halted for four days to make a new dugout.

Resuming their journey on March 15, the party made six kilometers before rising ground and "the roar of broken water announced that once more our course was checked by dangerous rapids." Rounding a bend, they saw the new obstacle, "a wide descent of white water, with an island in the middle, at the upper edge." This time Kermit was in the lead canoe, along with two *camaradas,* a pet dog, and a week's supply of boxed provisions. Reconnoitering the island to see if a descent could be made on the far side, Kermit suddenly found his canoe caught in a shifting whirlpool and carried broadside into the rapids.

The paddlers were unable to head into the current—the only possible way to navigate the rapids—and the boat took wave after wave of water, quickly filled, and overturned in the frothy current. One of the *camaradas* reached shore, but the other disappeared beneath the waters—his body was never recovered. The current beat Kermit's helmet down over his face, and his Winchester was torn from his grasp. In swift but quieter water he swam toward shore. Although his jacket hindered his strokes, he knew that he did not have the strength to take it off. An overhanging branch appeared on the shore, and "with the curious calm one feels when death is but a moment away," his father later wrote, "he realized that the utmost his failing strength could do was to reach the branch." Desperately clutching at the branch, Kermit was then barely able to pull himself ashore with his last reserve of energy. Swimming alongside Kermit, the dog also clambered onto dry land.

T.R. was naturally distraught. The fear of some such accident befalling his second son had been a nightmare all along; "it did not seem to me that I could bear to bring bad tidings . . . to his mother." A sign was erected: "In These Rapids Died Poor Simplicio." Looking for his lost canoe, Kermit discovered even worse rapids a couple of kilometers downstream.

"The morning of the 16th was dark and gloomy," wrote the Colonel. "Through sheets of blinding rain we left our camp of misfortune for another camp where misfortune also awaited us." While another portage was being made that day Colonel Rondon strolled with a dog into the forest. Running on ahead, the animal was suddenly felled by Indian arrows; although the natives were not seen, their hostile presence was cause for new alarm. And during the portage the new dugout was lost when the rope by which it was being lowered through the churning waters broke. With Indians undoubtedly lurking nearby, it was deemed unwise to tarry long enough to build new canoes. All the baggage, trimmed to the barest necessity, was loaded into the four remaining dugouts. Roosevelt, Dr. Cajazeira, and six *camaradas*—three with feet so swollen from insect bites that they could scarcely walk—embarked once more on the stream. Colonel Rondon, Lyra, Cherrie, Kermit, and the nine other *camaradas* marched in a single file along the bank. The boats had to be halted continually to allow the slower shore party to catch up. "It is doubtful if all our party ever reaches Manáos," George Cherrie wrote in his diary.

The expedition camped that night at a point where a major stream joined the Dúvida; Colonel Rondon named it the Rio Kermit, and during a ceremony the next morning to erect a marker on the tributary he pulled from his pocket orders from the Brazilian government formally christening the Dúvida the Rio Roosevelt. T.R. protested; he preferred the name that seemed so appropriate, the River of Doubt, "but my kind friends insisted otherwise, and it would have been churlish of me to object longer." Three cheers were given for the United States, for T.R., and for Kermit. Roosevelt proposed three cheers for Brazil, for Colonel Rondon, for Lyra, for the doctor, and finally for all the *camaradas*. Only Cherrie had not been cheered, an omission soon taken care of, "and the meeting broke up in high good humor."

Just above its juncture with the Dúvida, the tributary Rio Kermit plunged over a waterfall six to eight feet in height; in the pool below were a number of fish, two of which were caught and provided delicious eating. One of the *camaradas*, a Parecís Indian named Antonio, stated confidently that fish never came up rapids in which falls had to be jumped. The fish in the Rio Kermit indicated, therefore, that the party would find no more rapids steep enough to require overland portaging. "But the event showed that he was mistaken," T.R. later noted sadly. "The worst rapids were ahead of us."

On March 19 the party halted for three days to make two new dugouts. An Indian fishing village, from which the natives had obviously just fled, was discovered in the vicinity; and gifts—an axe, a knife, some strings of red beads—were left to show that the interlopers were friendly. During the pause the members of the expedition had plenty of time to speculate about the river they were following. There was no longer any doubt, Roosevelt concluded, that the Dúvida was a big river, one of major importance. It now seemed probable that either it must empty directly into the Madeira, near that river's juncture with the Amazon, or it became the Aripuanã (as T.R. spelled it, "Aripuanan"), another affluent of the Madeira—although the Aripuanã had never been judged such a large river. In the three weeks since embarking on the River of Doubt the expedition had covered only about 140 kilometers, travelling two kilometers for every one made northward, with a descent of some 124 meters. A river normally describes a parabola in its course, Roosevelt thought, with the steepest descent in the upper reaches. This led him to hope that they would not have to encounter so many and such difficult rapids in the future—a hope, he wrote, "destined to failure."

On March 22, once more with six dugouts so that all could ride, the expedition again started down the Dúvida. Within twenty minutes out

they struck rapids, a pattern that was to be monotonously repeated for the next three weeks, the men counting themselves fortunate when the rapids were gentle enough to allow them to lower the unloaded boats through the water so that they had only to carry the baggage overland. Roosevelt remained cheerful and optimistic: ". . . while we were actually on the river, paddling and floating downstream along the reaches of swift, smooth water, it was very lovely." The very rapids that were now making their navigation downstream so hazardous, he mused, one day "would drive electric trolleys up and down its whole length and far out on either side and run mills and factories, and lighten the labor on farms." Such a rich and fertile land should not be permitted "to lie as a tenantless wilderness, while there are such teeming swarms of human beings in the overcrowded, overpeopled countries of the Old World."

During these backbreaking weeks the six leaders had been eating only two meals a day, consuming each day the contents of one provision box packed in New York by Fiala (the *camaradas* carried separate rations); but now they made each box last a day and a half or even two days. Only when some large bird or monkey was shot, or a fish caught, was there really enough food. In the evenings the men from North America would sit around discussing what they would eat when they got home. Cherrie craved griddlecakes and maple syrup; Kermit dreamed of strawberries and cream; T.R. said that he would choose a mutton chop "with a tail to it!" In addition to the generally weakened condition of the entire party caused by short rations, two men were now down with jungle fever. For several days Cherrie was too weak to make entries in his diary.

At the end of March they discovered that they were crossing a range of mountains "about the height

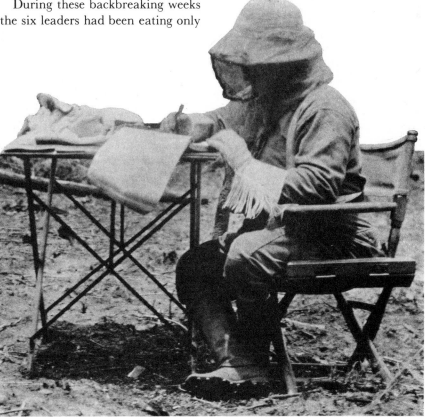

T.R. had to cover even his hands against insects when he did his daily stint of writing.

of the lower ridges of the Alleghenies." The river here entered a rapids three kilometers long that took them three days to portage; one kilometer below was another set of rapids that cost them an additional day. "We thought we had reduced our baggage before," T.R. wrote, "but now we cut to the bone." Kermit's shoes had finally given out, a casualty of so many hours spent in the water among the sharp rocks, and he took his father's spare pair. In addition to the clothes on his back the Colonel retained only one set of pajamas, one spare pair each of drawers and socks, half a dozen handkerchiefs, a wash kit, a pocket medicine case, and a little bag containing extra spectacles, needles and thread, gun grease, adhesive plaster, and his purse and a letter of credit to use at Manáos. T.R. still had a cot—the others were all sleeping on hammocks by then—but two tents were abandoned.

For this descent Rondon cut a trail for the *camaradas* to carry their burdens to the foot of the new rapids, while Kermit and Lyra, with four of the best watermen, worked the canoes down the gorge on rope. Because of the constant fear of hostile natives, someone had to stand guard with a loaded rifle. In four days, T.R. wrote of this effort, the party had "accomplished a work of incredible labor and of the utmost importance; for at the first glance it had seemed an absolute impossibility to avoid abandoning the canoes when we found that the river sank into a cataract-broken torrent at the bottom of a canyon-like gorge between steep mountains." Nonetheless, one dugout was lost.

On April 2 the expedition started out on the river once more, "wondering how soon we should strike other rapids in the mountains ahead, and whether in any reasonable time we should, as the aneroid [barometer] indicated, be so low down that we should necessarily be in a plain where

we could make a journey of at least a few days without rapids." For a month they had been descending an uninterrupted series of rapids. They had lost four of the seven canoes with which they had started and one of the three built en route, one man, and a dog, "which by its death had in all probability saved the life of Colonel Rondon." The *camaradas* were dispirited, occasionally asking one or more of the leaders if they thought they would ever get out of the jungle alive, "and we had to cheer them up as best we could." Reconnoitering ahead, Rondon, Lyra, and Kermit discovered yet another series of "sinister rapids."

"Under such conditions whatever is evil in men's natures comes to the front," T.R. wrote of the situation as they confronted the grueling portage. "On this day a strange and terrible tragedy occurred." One man alone of the original sixteen *camaradas* had proved worthless; he was a huge, surly man of European background named Julio. He constantly shirked tasks and had been caught stealing food on several occasions. At the outset of this day's portage one of the men accused Julio of stealing some dried meat, and a Negro corporal named Paishon rebuked him for lagging behind. Yet no one paid attention when Julio casually picked up a carbine and followed Paishon down the portage trail. A minute later a shot rang out, and three or four of the men ran back to say that Julio had killed Paishon and run off into the woods. The Colonel and the doctor tried to find the killer but shortly lost his track in the dense undergrowth; they feared he had gone amuck and would try to wipe out the entire party.

Paishon was simply and quickly buried along the portage trail where he had been slain. The expedition's cook noted that the corporal had fallen forward on his hands and knees, "and when a murdered man falls like that his ghost will follow the slayer as

long as the slayer lives." The party could not immediately stop to pursue Julio, but three days later he appeared on the bank and called out that he wished to surrender. Roosevelt feared that if the murderer were taken he would prove a menace to the party: they could ill afford to maintain a round-the-clock guard over him, and meanwhile he would be but an extra mouth to feed. Rondon, however, felt that it was his duty to bring the man back to civilization and to justice. But meantime the canoes had swept on past Julio, he had disappeared once more into the wilderness, and the two men sent back to take the murderer never found him.

In this tense situation the party had tried to hurry the dangerous portage and had lost another canoe. Jumping in the water to help with an overturned dugout, T.R. had badly bruised his leg; the resulting inflammation, he now wrote in deliberate understatement, "was somewhat bothersome." As luck would have it, the bruised leg was the one that had been seriously injured in a carriage accident in 1902, and Roosevelt developed what his son called "a veritable plague of deep abscesses." Doctor Cajazeira lanced the abscesses to relieve the inflammation and inserted a drainage tube. There was "an added charm" to this primitive operation, Roosevelt observed, in the enthusiasm with which the numerous insects "took part therein." But T.R.'s condition was not a matter to be taken lightly; concurrently he had a sharp attack of fever that completely debilitated him for the next forty-eight hours.

"The scene is vivid before me," Kermit later wrote of that night, as he and the doctor divided a watch over the delirious Roosevelt. "The black rushing river with the great trees towering high above along the bank; the sodden earth under foot; for a few moments the stars would be shining, and then the sky would cloud over and the rain would fall in torrents, shutting out sky and trees and river." T.R. started reciting poetry— *"In Xanadu did Kubla Khan / A stately pleasure dome decree...."* Then he would enter into an incoherent monologue, mostly focusing on the lack of supplies; he wondered if Kermit and Cherrie were getting enough food. "I can't work now," Kermit heard him say, "so I don't need much food, but he [Kermit] and Cherrie have worked all day with the canoes; they must have part of mine."

Colonel Rondon himself had nearly given in to despair; only that morning he had proposed that they abandon the canoes rather than attempt another portage and that the party fight its way out of the jungle on foot, "every man for himself." When he came out of his fever, T.R. called Cherrie and Kermit to his bedside. "Cherrie, I want you and Kermit to go ahead. We have reached a point where some of us must stop. I feel I am only a burden to the party." He had morphine in his kit and thought of ending his life there. But, he later told newspaperman O. K. Davis, he knew that his son would leave neither him nor his body in the jungle. "So there was only one thing for me to do, and that was to come out myself."

At this point, Cherrie later claimed, it was twenty-four-year-old Kermit who held the expedition together—working nearly naked in the water with the canoes, his legs cut and bruised and swollen with insect bites, suffering occasionally from attacks of fever himself. They finally got through the "sinister rapids" of the jungle homicide and out once more on the broad river, where the relentless sun, Kermit recalled, "hung above us all the day like a molten ball and broiled us as if the river were a grid on which we were made fast." To a sick man like his father, Kermit knew, the heat must have been intolerable.

"How I longed for a big Maine birchbark such as that in which I once went down the Mattawamkeag at high water!" T.R. wrote of his final days on the Dúvida. "It would have slipped down these rapids as a girl trips through a country-dance." But the pattern of brief runs on the wide river and long, laborious portagings around the numerous rapids continued through the first two weeks of April. Easter Sunday, April 12, was passed "in the fashion with which we were altogether too familiar," the Colonel recorded wearily, but late in the afternoon of the next day "the river began to run in long and quiet reaches." And the day after that they made fifteen kilometers; for the first time in several weeks they camped where they did not hear the sound of rapids. Fish were caught, a monkey and some birds that tasted like turkey were shot, and the *camaradas* gorged themselves on nuts—which unfortunately made them sick the next day. Thus it was "a sorry crew" that embarked on the morning of the fifteenth. "But it turned out a red-letter day."

The previous day the party had noted what seemed to be cuttings of rubber trees, perhaps a year old but very likely the work of pioneer rubbermen pressing into the wilderness. Two and a half hours out on April 15 they spied a board on a post with the initials "J.A."—evidently marking the farthest point upriver from the Amazon penetrated by a rubberman and claimed as his own. An hour after that they came upon a newly built house in a planted clearing, and all cheered heartily. "No one was at home, but the house of palm thatch was clean and cool. A couple of dogs were on watch, and the belongings showed that a man and a woman and a child lived there and had only just left." An hour later a second house was sighted and they were welcomed to it by "an old black man who showed the innate courtesy of the Brazilian peasant," T.R. wrote. Civi-

lization, however rude, had been reached; and the Dúvida proved to be what these frontier rubbermen called the Castanho, an affluent or western branch of the Aripuanã, which eventually flowed into the Madeira and thus led to the Amazon. Henceforth they would be following a river that, if still not on any maps, was at least known to men of the wilderness.

"It was time to get out," T.R. concluded. "The wearing work, under very unhealthy conditions, was beginning to tell on every one." Half the *camaradas* had been down with the fever; and although Kermit and Cherrie had recovered from their attacks of fever, the younger Roosevelt and Lyra suffered greatly from bleeding sores on their legs, sores that had developed from the bruises incurred during the river work. The Colonel, at last, could admit that he himself was in bad shape—from the fever and from the abscesses on his injured leg. But the worst was past, and the "north was calling strongly...." At nightfall they could see the Big Dipper well above the horizon—"upside down, with the two pointers pointing to a north star below the world's rim; but the Dipper, with all its stars." At Sagamore Hill, he knew, spring had come, "the wonderful northern spring of long glorious days, of brooding twilights, of cool delightful nights." Each of the three North Americans—Cherrie, Kermit, and the Colonel—"was longing for the homely things that were so dear to him, for the home people who were dearer still, and for the one who was dearest of all."

"Our adventures and our troubles alike were over," T.R. wrote of their last two weeks on the Rio da Dúvida. A rubberman was hired as a guide; and even though there were additional rapids to traverse, "it was all child's play compared to what we had gone through." Their guide could tell them what lay ahead, and trails for portaging had been blazed around the worst rapids; soon they were making fifty kilometers a day. On April 27—exactly two months after embarking on the River of Doubt—the Expedição Scientifica Roosevelt-Rondon reached the hamlet of São João. A three-day journey downstream aboard a river steamer brought them to Manáos, where they learned that the two other parties had come out safely down the Tapajós and Gy-Paraná rivers. Leo Miller later recalled that Colonel Roosevelt, by the time of his arrival at the river city, "had wasted to a mere shadow of his former self; but his unbounded enthusiasm remained undiminished." The young naturalist was sorry that Fiala had already left for New York and could not record the arrival at Manáos on motion-picture film—as he had the expedition's departure overland from Tapirapuan three months earlier; "the two pictures side by side would have told an interesting story."

"We have had a hard and somewhat dangerous but very successful trip," T.R. wired the Brazilian minister of foreign affairs, General Müller, from Manáos on April 30. He briefly recounted the expedition's tribulations but then triumphantly recorded that they had "put on the map a river about 1500 kilometers in length running from just south of the 13th degree to north of the 5th degree and the biggest affluent of the Madeira." Roosevelt concluded, "My dear Sir, I thank you from my heart for the chance to take part in this great work of exploration."

At Manáos, Roosevelt said good-bye to the thirteen remaining *camaradas*, giving each some gold sovereigns—one of which, he later learned, each man kept as a token of his journey with the famous North American. An Amazon steamer took the rest of the party to Pará, or Belém, where final farewells were said between the Brazilians and the Americans. Together with his admiration for the "hardihood, courage, and resolution" of Rondon, Lyra, and Doc-

tor Cajazeira, Roosevelt confessed to a "strong and affectionate friendship for them"; he was glad to have "been their companion in the performance of a feat which possessed a certain lasting importance."

"The Brazilian Wilderness," wrote William Roscoe Thayer, a historian and Roosevelt's friend, "stole away ten years of his life." Corinne Roosevelt Robinson claimed that her brother returned from the trip "a man in whom a secret poison still lurked"; he was never thereafter "wholly free from recurrent attacks of

Though ill, aged, and thinner, T.R. could still joke with newsmen on his return home.
THEODORE ROOSEVELT BIRTHPLACE, NEW YORK

the terrible jungle fever. . . ." Passengers on the liner *Aidan* were shocked by the Colonel's appearance when he came aboard at Belém on May 7; he was thin and gaunt and subject to frequent attacks of fever. But his appetite soon picked up. At Bridgetown, Barbados, where the ship stopped, he purchased fifty books and, sitting in the sun on deck each day, read them all before the *Aidan* reached New York on May 19.

When the liner stopped at quaran-

tine shortly before four that afternoon, a tug pulled up; aboard were the ex-President's wife, Edith, and two other sons, Theodore, Jr., and Archie. Two additional tugs carried photographers and reporters. Passing in the channel was the *Hamburg*, which had borne the Colonel across the Atlantic in 1909 on a trip to Africa; she signalled a greeting with three whistles and disappeared into open waters. The newspapermen were dismayed to see how thin and old the Bull Moose hero looked; "Roosevelt Returns 35 Pounds Lighter," the *New York Times* headlined its story about the arrival. Side by side the paper ran "before" and "after" pictures of the Colonel. The *Times* writer described T.R. as being "thinner and older looking, and there was something lacking in the power of his voice. His face had a hearty color, but there were lines that were not there before." Yet, the reporter concluded, "none of the old time vivacity of manner was lacking." Calling attention himself to the cane he was leaning heavily on, T.R. joked, ". . . you see I still have the big stick."

Roosevelt indeed had some political weight in the United States—and an interesting few years ahead. Although he declined the Bull Moose nomination for governor of New York later in 1914, he rejoined the Republican Party in 1916 and unsuccessfully sought the Presidential nomination. When World War I broke out in Europe, he led the crusade against neutrality and for American preparedness but was refused permission by Wilson to raise and lead a cavalry division to France after the United States entered the conflict. By the end of 1918, with the war over and with Wilson's leadership repudiated in the midterm elections, the Colonel was once more hailed as the leader of the G.O.P. and was being widely discussed as a virtually unbeatable candidate for President in 1920. About 4 A.M. on January 6, 1919, at Sagamore Hill, Theodore Roosevelt died in his sleep of a pulmonary embolism. He had turned sixty only two months earlier.

No question about it. The subject matter that I devoted my art to has practically disappeared. Not wholly, because I know areas where I could go out and live on a farm and refind it. But generally speaking, it's a dying culture. It's gone. And one thing about it, the town near that farm today will be just like any other town. I have really sort of lost my subject matter.

How did your assignment to do the New School mural come about?

Well, I can tell you about that. It was in 1928, I think, that Alma Reed opened the Delphic gallery in New York, largely to promote the work of the Mexican muralist José Clemente Orozco. I don't know how far I should go with that, because the relations between Alma and Orozco, well, they were not just dealer and artist at all. At any rate, Clemente had seen my historical murals and liked them, and I was the only American artist he wanted in the gallery with him. So I agreed. The main problem was to find wall space for our murals, and it was Alma's contention that we'd have to work cheaply at first to get started.

Did you agree with her?

No. But as it turned out, she was right. What happened was that when she heard about the construction of the New School, she went and negotiated a mural for Orozco and not me. Now, when this got out, there were a number of people, like Lewis Mumford and particularly Ralph Pierson, who was quite well-known in New York art circles, who were furious. Pierson himself went to Alvin Johnson, the director of the New School, and said it was an outrage that someone like me, who had worked so hard to develop a new American mural style, was to be excluded from the project. So Dr. Johnson promised me a wall to paint if I would work on the same terms as Orozco had.

What terms were those?

I worked for nothing. The New School paid the paint expenses.

Did this lead to a break with Alma Reed and the Delphic gallery?

Well, yeah. Not an open break, but it wasn't pleasant anymore, and I quit her shortly after.

Did Orozco have any specific influence on you at this time?

None, except that I liked his work, and he liked mine, although I don't think he did after my painting began to

be highly localized. You see, Orozco, unlike Diego Rivera, always dealt in what are called universal symbols. Clemente's original works, like mine, were very much influenced by Michelangelo. That's probably why he liked my early murals.

In your murals, how do you decide which elements you want to include?

You mean the subject matter? Well, there are two different ways. In the historical murals the images are all based upon verbal accounts, of course. In the New School mural I had by then done so much sketching in the field that I was ready and anxious for an opportunity to put some of this new stuff into a form. I had already done one modern thing, called the *Bootleggers*, and I was more and more fascinated with modern subjects. So when the New School thing came up, Alvin Johnson and I decided to concentrate on contemporary America, and I had the material in my travel sketchbooks, all of it. It was simply a question of organizing it.

I know that Rita and your infant son, T.P., both posed for the New School mural, but I also noticed that in one corner panel you yourself are pictured talking to Dr. Johnson.

Yeah. We are both drinking whiskey, showing that we were what they called scofflaws during Prohibition. I recall that Johnson was a bit leery at first about the whiskey, but he was a man with a good sense of humor. As far as the artist putting himself in his painting, that's not new. Giotto did it, Signorelli did it, lots of painters did it.

When the New School mural was unveiled in 1931, it raised a storm of protest from both radical and conservative art circles. Had you anticipated this kind of reaction?

Hell, no. I thought I had made something that was going to please *everybody*.

The conservatives didn't like your use of contemporary subject matter, whereas the radicals were furious that there was no ideological protest in your mural. Were you under any kind of pressure to inject a Marxist viewpoint?

Oh, yes. Quite a bit—from my associates at the time and through my connection with certain Marxist groups like the People's Art Guild and the Barnhouse group here on Martha's Vineyard. I was, at one time, a quite convinced Marxist, but I never joined any of the societies or parties that were propagating those ideas. In fact, by 1928 I had completely lost faith in the efficacy of Marxism in the United States.

You turned from Marxism in 1928? That was well before it became so fashionable for artists and writers. Was this because of your extensive family background in politics?

None of them had my kind of background. They were innocents. I had known enough politics to know that while Marxist theory was itself logical and quite convincing, there was always the political business, the question of power. And I was proved right later, with the rise of Stalin. Although you may have a theoretical good in mind, the means that are used to attain it have a hell of an effect on it.

A*re you glad now that you didn't get more deeply involved in the Marxist movement?*

I got enough involved as it was, so that I was under surveillance for a while. When Bob Minor was active in the Communist Party, under the Palmer regime, when Attorney General Palmer was pursuing everybody in New York, I let Minor have our apartment for a meeting of the Communist Party. And of course that was found out and got in the hands of people in Missouri and used to lambaste me with there.

How would you describe yourself today politically?

I'm a very conservative man, always have been. I've tied myself to the traditions of the Western world in which I was raised, and have tried to perform within them. I've no idea to revolutionize anything. I know things are going to be revolutionized without me. It may well be that we've come to the end of the capitalist world, which has produced more freedom for the individual than any other system in history, but maybe too damned much. I don't know. But it does seem evident to me that we're not going to have nineteenth-century capitalism last through the twentieth, although if you say that, they call you a Commie, which is absurd.

You seem to have been called just about everything in your career, from opportunistic to anti-Semitic.

That anti-Semitism business was started by some of the young Jewish idealists who controlled the John Reed Club of New York. They used that charge to beat me with because I wouldn't put a lot of Marxist propaganda in my murals, but that accusation died out with the fracas. The other names I was called didn't bother me especially, although I did object to being called an opportunist. Still do.

How could you afford to paint the New School mural for nothing, by the way?

I got five hundred dollars for teaching that winter at the New School, and the Whitney Museum bought all the preliminary sketches. And then the Whitney considered buying a series of big sketches I had made for the rotunda of the New York Public Library, which had been rejected. But Mrs. Juliana Force, the director of the Whitney, decided that it would be better if I made a new mural for the museum's library, and so they advanced me four thousand dollars. But when I finished the mural, they only paid one thousand dollars more, and I was so disappointed I got drunk at the opening and gave the thousand back. That was the last time I ever worked without a contract, and that was the beginning of the hard feelings between me and the Whitney.

Is it true that when the Whitney moved in 1956 to its new quarters, the museum actually offered to give you back the mural?

I was shocked when they repudiated it. I gave it to the museum in Bridgeport, Connecticut.

The Whitney mural, I understand, had already aroused a lot of criticism, including a very hostile round-robin letter from your co-instructors at the Art Students League.

I don't know what went on in the minds of those fellows to make them do that. Frankly, I do not know what occasioned the general animosities, either.

Do you think they were envious of you?

You mean at the attention I was getting? I can't see that, since nearly all of it was adverse. And it couldn't have been envy of my talent, because all of them were better artists than I was, and told me so. It's curious, though. Even my friend E. E. Cummings, who was an amateur painter, got quite nasty and satirical toward me. He addressed me always as "the great American painter," and I soon got tired of that and quit seeing him. I guess I can understand a little bit, because in those murals I broke with those aesthetic groups who were inspired largely by what was going on in Paris, and with the Marxists, the social realists who believed that art should be put at the service of the proletarian revolution. I fitted with neither of them, and things got quite violent. But then, everything was violent in the 1930's.

Your friend Thomas Craven once wrote that because of the "raw-hide individualism" of your painting, you do not fit into any of the ready-made categories of modern art.

Maybe I don't. But I'm tied in many ways. I've been influenced all my life by this, that, and the other school. And I can't say that there is anything that I have invented in any of my art. All I've discovered was what was within reach of anybody in America. "Red" [Sinclair] Lewis, [William] Faulkner, Sherwood Anderson, Tennessee Williams—they all discovered the same thing I did.

Are those your favorite authors?

Mark Twain, of course. Those were the first stories I ever read, that and the *Arabian Nights*, and I still read both.

You don't seem to have ever gone out of your way to avoid controversy, any more than your famous great-uncle did. Is this a Benton family trait?

Well, that will be your comparison. I'm not imitating him or trying to. I'm going to tell you about this, though. Let's get it clean. I'm not just looking to assert myself in my art. I'm not hunting my own soul. I was really trying to present America, and I thought I had a fairly objective view of it. Of course, as you pointed out, there was romance in it, but it was not the kind of romance that was always acceptable everywhere.

What was your next mural project after the Whitney?

I contracted to paint the Indiana state mural for the exposition in Chicago in June, 1933.

Was that the mural that caused such a storm because you included the Ku Klux Klan in it?

Yeah. Now there was a case. . . . You asked me earlier whether being named Thomas Hart Benton had affected my career. . . . My name was a great assistance in the case of the Indiana mural. Indiana was the first very large commission I got. And my entrée into the political area, which was necessary to confirm the contract, was definitely made possible by my name, because the Democratic politicos who controlled the state regarded me as a brother and not just a damned New York artist. And the same was true a few years later in Missouri, where I was able to override any controversies, control my contract, subject matter, and everything else, very largely because of my name.

Let's talk about the Missouri State House mural, which you finished in 1936. How would you rate it among all your murals?

If I have any right to make judgments, I would say that the Missouri mural was my best work. I was thoroughly matured. I had had the Indiana experience, and I knew what to do. Plus, I knew what kind of contract to demand.

What kind of contract was that?

It was put through the Missouri legislature by Senator Edward Barbour, a friend of my brother's, and mine, too. Barbour managed somehow, I don't know how, to get the bill through, authorizing the mural and sixteen thousand dollars to pay for it, without entangling me in any way with the then dominant [Thomas] Pendergast machine. But there was a clause in it that I must work under state art supervision. Well, I had watched all the problems that the politicians had caused in the art projects of the WPA, and so I telegraphed from New York and told them that I wouldn't sign the contract unless they removed that clause. That was demanding a good deal, but they did it. And the only reason they did it was because all those goddamned state politicians had a great admiration for my father, and respected the Benton family name.

How do you feel about the criticism over your depiction of Boss Pendergast and the saga of Frankie and Johnny in the Missouri mural?

I believe that the myths of a country picture it almost, well, practically better than its damned politics. As far as Pendergast was concerned, I told him that this was to be a mural of contemporary Missouri, and what the hell, it can't be complete without you, and he agreed that that was true. So he posed for me in his Kansas City office. He wanted to be in it or he wouldn't have posed. There wasn't any trouble about it at all.

The trouble came afterward?

Later on, after Pendergast got to the penitentiary, some wag went up and painted his prison number on his back in the mural, and somebody told Harry Truman that I had done that. And that caused considerable coldness between Truman and me for years, until he actually got to know me and realized that I wouldn't have done such a thing. I remember when I first met him in the White

House, he said to me then, "Are you still making those controversial pictures?" And I think I replied, "I would if I could get some more of them to do."

What did you mean afterward when you said you were astounded by the "conventional nature" of the criticism that was levelled at the Missouri mural?

I did? I don't remember saying that. You see, all the time I was painting, I left that room wide open, and all the people of the state who had business in Jefferson City could come in and watch. About the only adverse comments I heard the whole time would be an occasional complaint from some farmer about some detail, and sometimes they were right, and I would change it. Now the general public in Missouri liked that mural and still do. It was only a small cultivated public in St. Louis and Kansas City that raised that fracas. Supposedly cultivated. Stupid as hell. And certain politicians, like Matt Murray, the state engineer, who said publicly, "I wouldn't hang a Benton on my s——house wall." So it wasn't the public that protested. It was a just a bunch of machine politicians and the polite element of society, mostly Republicans.

Your contract in 1935 to paint the Missouri mural coincided with your moving to Kansas City to join the faculty of the art institute there. Since you had been turned down by the institute in 1912, was this sort of a triumphant homecoming?

No. I've never told the real reason. I was up in Kansas City on a Christmas buying trip in 1912, and I ran into a fellow I'd known back in Chicago. He had been a teacher in Chicago when I was a student there. Well, he said that the art institute in Kansas City needed a man who had just returned from Paris—only it turned out that they were all homosexuals in the place, and I didn't get along.

This was in Kansas City in 1912?

At that time Kansas City was a vaudeville and carnival exchange center, and it was a place where the chorus boys would be stranded for weeks at a time. And somehow or other, Kansas City had become a quite developed homosexual center in 1912, and it had reached into the art institute. Now listen, I'd been through Paris, and I'd never seen anything like that. It shocked the hell out of me. They had a party for me, and they all came in women's underwear and all that stuff. This was something I was absolutely innocent about, and I couldn't stay there.

Before you left New York in 1935, didn't you sound off about the "precious fairies" who dominated the art world and who, you complained, were inhibiting the development of a truly American art form?

I said that, and for a while I was persona non grata in every art museum in the country because of that statement. I'm trying to just soft-pedal that now, because they've sort of come around to me, in spite of that. They have to, in a way. But what I said then is, if anything, even stronger today. These homosexuals are quite influential in this particular game I'm in. In fact, they control it. You get a reputation as an artist with their permission.

Do you think it's a question of temperament, of injecting effeminate attitudes toward art?

It's not necessarily effeminate, it's precious. It's the Oscar Wilde attitude toward art that they bring. And that's something I don't like. You see, they are nearly all highly in favor of the more abstract movements, where they can seem to belong to an elite group. As a matter of fact, the success of the various abstract movements in the United States has largely depended upon the promotion of these homosexuals. Let me put it this way. In every field there's always some son of a bitch who "knows" what nobody else knows, and he don't know it, but he rests his fame on it. You have the same thing in the art world. If you get something that no one else can understand and you understand it or can convince others that you understand it, that puts you in a superior position.

And you still feel that this "precious" influence hurts American art?

I'm quite sure it does. You see, when only women and homosexuals are interested in the arts, it shows that the arts don't have much of a place in the culture. Their influence has the effect of withdrawing art from its public function. They want it to be their own precious domain.

That's really the essence of your central premise, isn't it, that art must have a social function?

Some kind. It's healthy. It's always had through history, and when it doesn't have now, you feel that there is degeneration. Maybe its social function is played out. Maybe this is the end. I don't know. There seems to be more public attention to art now in this country than ever before, but it still doesn't seem to perform any function or communicate much. Today we do have the cowboy-and-Indian art in the West, which has attracted a great following, and the advertising arts. But advertising degrades art, and the western stuff is so obviously a romantic resuscitation that it isn't contemporary at all. This western art never gives you the sense of any kind of change. There are no more Indians riding around on lonely peaks anymore, and if there are, they've got a can of beer in their hand instead of a spear.

Didn't you try your hand at advertising art in the late 1930's?

At that time I was very optimistic about a possible marriage between commerce and art, but I found out after a few months that it was impossible. The advertising people were too damned sensitive about the subject matter, although they continued to use some of the paintings I made for the American Tobacco Company for quite a while. Lewenthal got me into that.

Reeves Lewenthal, was he the man who started the Associated American Artists?

Yeah. Lewenthal was a regular entrepreneur, with quite a stable of artists, including myself and Wood and Curry. Regionalism was already pretty strong when he took us on, but there is no question that he did a very effective job of popularizing the Americanist artists, including some of the boys from the John Reed Club who had graduated from their former hatred of the regionalist movement. And Lewenthal brought money in, especially with his five-dollar lithographs, which sold in the thousands.

When did you make your famous caustic remark about preferring to hang your paintings in saloons and whorehouses, where normal people could see them?

Benton (at left) with his Persephone, *which he painted in 1939*

It was in 1939, when Lewenthal opened his Fifth Avenue gallery, and I exhibited two nude studies, *Susanna and the Elders* and *Persephone,* which caused some controversy, although I'm not really sure why. I did the same thing that's been done through history, the same thing as Giorgione's *Fête Champêtre,* in which the men have the costume of the day, although the women, of course, don't have any costumes at all. *Susanna* was rather specifically done, with some pubic hair showing, and that resulted in a bit of a furor that seems absurd today. At any rate the reporters used to come to my openings, and we'd get drunk and get to talking about everything. Well, I made that remark about saloons and whorehouses, and the next day a fellow from the old New York *Telegram* came to me and asked me if I would stand by it. And I said, yeah. I wasn't going to back down.

D*idn't the publication of that remark cost you your teaching job at the Kansas City Art Institute?*

That was the reason they gave, but I was having a lot of trouble there with the trustees. They tried to get me to resign, but I made them fire me. And it was good for me, too. It was taking too much time that I needed for painting. At the time they thought they had me in an economic wringer, but they didn't know I was doing pretty well.

What sort of trouble were you having with the trustees?

Well, the main thing was that the trustees had decided they wanted an accredited school, so they could give degrees, and they wanted me to grade the students. I wouldn't do it. I wanted to run it as a regular old-fashioned art school and not as a goddamned adjunct to a college. I also would not engage in the school's social activities. And politically, all the trustees were very strong conservative Republicans, more conservative than you can imagine, and everything that seemed to come up, well, we disagreed on. I was glad to get out.

The regionalist school of painting really fell out of favor with the coming of World War II, didn't it?

Well, you must remember, the regionalist movement, not only in the United States but in Mexico and Germany and even in Italy, to name just a few, had actually dominated the scene for nearly twenty years. But it is true that the war . . . actually, both wars had the same effect of emptying art of content. That's something a sociologist or psychologist ought to look into.

89

How did the public rejection of regionalism affect your colleagues Wood and Curry?

Much more deeply than I. They cared more. Having had fewer controversies than I had, Wood and Curry were probably more sensitive to the criticism of the movement and more easily hurt by it. And neither one of them being highly verbal, I'm sure they took verbal statements much more seriously than I would.

When you visited Grant Wood on his deathbed in 1942, were you shocked when he told you he intended to change his name and start all over again as a painter?

I didn't take it very seriously. I considered it a state of his illness.

But he had lost confidence in his art?

Completely.

Was the same thing true of Curry before his death in 1946?

It was. Of course, Curry was suffering from high blood pressure, and that in itself was a depressant. But he was always immensely subject to criticism. From the very beginning he used to cry over it. Great big buck, you know. Seems sort of odd. On the other hand, those periods of depression—the sense of rejection and the uselessness of your effort—I think every artist must have them at some time. I had a number of them, but I always got over them. And I'm sure Jack Pollock had it before he died. His last three years, you know, he didn't do anything and was in a terribly depressed state.

Pollock was more than just your most famous student. For many years he was practically a member of your family. Did it upset you when he said that your chief value to him as a painter consisted of someone to react against?

Jack never said that to me. I think it was one of the many things that were put in his mouth by the critics. And there was really no occasion for Jack to say anything like that. He had made his own departure as an artist. I haven't repudiated any of my influences. I admit them all. I don't give a damn.

Doesn't it seem ironic that the best-known student of a famous representational painter should acquire his reputation as an abstract expressionist?

It seems like a natural reaction to me. You talk about sons rejecting their fathers. Well, he was practically a son.

Pollock died in 1956. It was the following year that you were first approached about the proposed mural for the Truman Library in Independence. Would you tell me about your relations with the former President?

It was a late acquaintanceship, and there isn't very much to say, except that I got along with him. I had no adventures with him, no arguments. I have enormous respect for him, of course. But as I told you, after that Pendergast thing with the Missouri mural, he was rather cold to me when I met him in Washington. In fact, Truman was not originally in favor of my doing his mural. I rather suspect that in the beginning he was a little afraid I was going to do something controversial on his library wall.

Did the President go over each detail of the mural with you?

No. We knew from the beginning what the subject matter was to be. The question always was whether Harry would be in the mural. The Washington crowd that raised the money, they wanted him in it. I knew this was going to be a problem, so I was going to treat him as a spectator, much in the way the old paintings used to include the donors, you know. But Harry refused to be in it, and I was very glad of it. I admired him for it, too. He was very cautious at first about giving me control of the subject matter, but he finally gave in, and he said time and again publicly that I did him a great favor. We got to be very great personal friends while I was doing that mural. The day I started painting it I even got him to climb up on the scaffold with me and paint the first strokes of the sky for the news cameras.

In May, 1962, shortly after the Truman Library mural was unveiled, your hometown of Neosho held a special "homecoming" celebration for you.

President Truman did me the honor of attending that affair, and we all rode down to Neosho from Kansas City on the President's private railroad car with Harry and his wife, Bess. And when we got there, there were flags and signs and a big cheering crowd, so I turned to the President and, because he was our greatest Missourian, I suggested that he go out first. But he said it was my day, and he pushed me out the door. That was so typical of the President.

That must have been a pretty exciting occasion.

Yeah, I'll tell you. I had a hard time taking that. ☆

The Chocolate Camelot

CONTINUED FROM PAGE 10

caramels, Milton was stoned by competing vendors who wanted him out of their territory, and the future looked black until an English candy importer chanced to spot Hershey, sample his wares, and order a large shipment. Although all his uncles were down on him for his past failures, Hershey somehow convinced the Lancaster National Bank to lend him seventeen hundred dollars for new equipment and supplies, and once more Aunt Mattie and his mother found themselves wrapping caramels for Milton. The English exports paid off handsomely, and Hershey's business was at long last on its way to success. With his various caramels—the ten-for-a-penny bean-shaped McGinties and the Jim Cracks, Roly Polies, and Lotuses—Hershey expanded his Lancaster Caramel Company locally as well as to plants in New York and Chicago until by 1894 he was doing a million dollars of business a year and owned the world's largest caramel factory. If there hadn't been a much bigger one ahead, this first poor-boy-makes-good story of Hershey's single-decade success would already have made a passable American legend.

But with some of the same feisty spirit that informed Israel Putnam's Bunker Hill command "Don't fire until you see the whites of their eyes!"—and we are indeed blessed that there always seems to be somebody around to jot down these inspired remarks—Milton Hershey made a vow out loud when he visited the 1893 World's Columbian Exposition in Chicago and got his first look at some of the machinery for roasting, hulling, grinding, mixing, and molding chocolate being displayed by the J. M. Lehmann firm of Dresden. Hershey's proclamation, made to a cousin who went out to the fair with him, was "Frank, I'm going to make chocolate!" Within weeks the Lancaster plant was full of Germans installing the new chocolate-making machinery. "Caramels are only a fad," said Hershey, swept up in his new enthusiasm. Soon chocolate candies were pouring out of the plant, and some of the caramels, which continued as the mainstay of production, were sporting chocolate coats.

There were chocolate cigarettes called Le Chat Noir, Smart Set, and Tennis; chocolate cigars called Hero of Manila; and chocolate chrysanthemums, lobsters, and bicycles. There were vanilla chocolate cakes, chocolate wafers, fruit tablets, bricks, croquettes, batons, ladyfingers, even chocolate midgets and chocolate dominoes. Although made in the caramel plant, the new candy was put out in wrappers that bore, somewhere, the legend Hershey's Chocolate. Aunt Mattie died before the new specialties began paying off, but Hershey did buy a new house for his mother and himself on Queen Street, in

Lancaster, and installed a fountain that had a silver ball balanced on a jet of water, out in the front garden. Inside there were flocks of birds in cages, a new $700 Swiss music box, and a new $580 hall clock on an onyx base. He also hired a coachman in livery.

Although Hershey's involvements with his mother and his aunt have been diligently traced by contemporaries who wrote about him, nobody ever said anything—for the record, anyway—about his love life. But in 1898, all by himself, without either his father or mother in attendance, Hershey married an Irish candy-store clerk from New York in St. Patrick's Cathedral. Her name was Catherine Sweeney, and he took her home to live with him and his mother on Queen Street. This little household was a disaster from the start—mother and wife "don't get on together at all," Hershey told a friend—so he bought his mother another house and hired her a companion. For good measure he bought the old farmhouse in Derry Township that he was born in and set his father up in that. It was at this point of the neat arranging of the various parts of his life that Hershey faced a new threat: the American Caramel Company wanted him to merge with them in order to make an American caramel monopoly, and if he refused, they would run him out of business. Hershey refused, so American changed its tune and offered to buy him out.

The idea appealed to Hershey if he could keep the chocolate end of the business to himself, so—after some wheeling and dealing—he sold the Lancaster Caramel Company, in 1900, for exactly one million dollars in cash. "That was the best business deal I ever made," Hershey told a friend. He did indeed keep his chocolate business, renting a wing of his former plant. Celebrating, he decided to take his wife and his mother on a trip around the world, but by the time they got to Mexico City, they were tired of it. Reported Hershey: "Mrs. Hershey said to me, 'If you call this having a good time, it is more than I do, and I would welcome going back home.' As these were exactly my sentiments, we cancelled the round-the-world trip and returned to Lancaster." The following year Hershey, then forty-four years old, sold $622,000 worth of chocolate. It was time to expand again, and Milton Hershey responded to the challenge, this time, with a visionary dream. Instead of just a new factory he would build a whole new town—a utopia. In the beauty and perfection of his community the dismal bleakness of all the typical Pennsylvania company towns, run by the mines and mills, would be erased. Hershey had left school in the fourth grade, but this was 1901, the quintessential moment of the self-made man, and Hershey was serenely confident that he could build a utopia as well as anybody else in the world.

For his new town Hershey bought twelve hundred acres of farmland near his birthplace in Derry Township, and ground was broken for the plant in 1903. The surrounding dairy land would provide milk for a fast-growing new product, milk chocolate in a bar. (This had been invented in Switzerland in 1876; Hershey's innovation was to take it out of the luxury class, sell it for a nickel, and make a national pastime out of eating Hershey bars.) He laid out Chocolate Avenue and Cocoa Avenue and built new houses for his workers to rent or to buy as they moved in from the closed-down operations in Lancaster. He built a hundred-room hotel and established the Hummelstown and Campbelltown Electric Street Railway, running between the plant and five surrounding towns. He built a pavilion in a park and put on free vaudeville shows and dances (music by the Hershey band), and there were restaurants, a lake with rowboats, baseball and football teams, new schools, a zoo, an amusement park, and a new railroad station. By 1906 Hershey, whose sales that year were already $1,200,000, was ready to name his utopia, so he held a naming contest. Suggestions included Chococoa City, Etabit, Qualitytells, Ulikit, Thrift, Hustletown, and even St. Milton. The prize went to a lady in Wilkes-Barre, for Hersheykoko, but the United States Post Office rejected this winner and shortened it to Hershey. Hershey was satisfied with that.

In 1908 Hershey incorporated his business, naming William F. R. Murrie, his long-time plant manager in Lancaster, as president. Hershey never did hold this title, keeping away from direct operational control as chairman of the board. In this year he also built High Point, a twenty-room mansion with a high, columned façade looking out complacently on the tall factory smokestacks a few hundred yards away. In the house he placed "tree-style" chandeliers from Paris, fourteen oil paintings from New York, and, although he was never seen reading a book, glassed-in bookcases with sets of classic authors. High Point was actually not enormously luxurious, however, and by the following year Hershey realized he was making more money than he knew what to do with, in spite of continuous expansion of the chocolate plant. The wealth, he decided, would go into an orphan school to be run right in Hershey, and for this purpose he bought 486 more acres of farmland. It would be a rather special school: it admitted principally boys with one parent—preferably a mother—still living. As for girls, they were not admitted at all. "The orphan boy has a hard time of it," said Hershey. "There are always relatives or outsiders who will take orphan girls, for they are useful in the home, and people are glad to get them. Boys are likely to be looked upon as a nuisance, and the more spirit they have the bigger nuisance they are, from that standpoint. So I want to help these boys." The plant would benefit slightly from the milk the boys would produce in their farming operation—Hershey always loved multipurpose enterprises—and the boys would learn farming and other useful trades only: "We do not plan to turn out a race of professors," said Hershey.

Like the factory, the orphan school prospered, and at length, in 1918, Hershey gave it all the stock—full ownership—of the Hershey Chocolate Company. Hershey's rather fawning biographer, his cousin Joseph R. Snavely, wrote that his hero was "as friendly a millionaire as one would wish to meet. He is of medium weight and height, and ruddy faced, with a grim, practical jaw that belies the twinkle in his eye. He talks slowly, and not so much at a time." He was also curious, willful, and suspicious and would poke around his town just as his mother had constantly patrolled the early family farmstead, looking for anything that might be out of place or in need of repair. Hershey would advise local residents—his employees, of course—to paint up a fence or clean up an untidy yard, and he once got thrown out of the local ice-cream parlor (Hershey-owned, too) when he snooped behind the counter to check on the cleanliness of the milk cans; the soda jerk did not know who he was. All municipal concerns were taken care of by the firm, and he would fire street laborers on the spot for leaning on their shovels. Once on an inspection tour of his hotel he spotted an unbeautiful sight through the open door of one of the rooms and barked in his high-pitched, impatient voice to the manager: "What are those pop bottles doing on the window in there?"

Examples of Hershey humor are rare. Says Sam Rosenberger, who retired from the firm in 1972, after forty-nine years as a cocoa-bean expert: "Hershey was a businessman, that came first with him. He never would spend time just talking with people or meeting them." A hint of Hershey whimsy did come out when an English manufacturer, visiting the Pennsylvania factory, claimed he could prove his own chocolate was better just by tasting it. Hershey managed to switch the labels on the samples, and when the Englishman claimed his victory, Hershey exposed the trick. On another occasion, when a union official tried to browbeat Hershey by insisting that no American should buy any nonunion product whatever, Hershey, on a hunch, bet him that his shirt was made by nonunion labor and proved he was right by exposing the label in the collar. He was not exactly self-effacing, but he was shy before groups and never made a speech of more than a few phrases. He hated telephones and would not have one in his office, and although his signature appeared on the Hershey bar—"none genuine without this signature"—for many years, he seldom signed documents or letters, preferring telegrams or simple oral instructions.

Hershey paid fair wages, but there were no advanced labor practices connected with his utopia—no paid vacations, medical care, or guaranteed wage. There were of course the free entertainment and the low tax rate in the town. Once in a while Hershey would run across a worthy object of help, and secretly, like George Arliss in *The Millionaire,* he would pay for everything needed. In one case it was a clubfooted boy who, Hershey was assured, could walk again with the help of the proper operations. Another local boy fell victim to some schoolmates who injured him severely in what was intended as a prank; Hershey took care, again, of all the bills. But while the charity was rare, the snooping was regular. One day, for example, Hershey noticed a haystack strangely in place in a field near his factory long after all the rest of the hay had been baled up and stowed in the barns for the winter. He poked into it and discovered a whole batch of spoiled chocolate his workers had hidden for lack of any better place to dump it. Two men were fired. Another time Hershey ordered a man to quit fishing in the town park. The culprit, who happened to be the town barber, gave Hershey some sass, so Hershey simply had the man's shop—which of course Hershey owned—hauled away.

As business improved—there was five million dollars' worth in 1911—Hershey simplified his line. Where he had had a hundred fourteen different chocolate items back in Lancaster, now he relied mainly on breakfast cocoa, chocolate syrup, and the mainstays, the bars, some now with almonds. The chocolate factory had turned into a money factory, practically running itself, and the main fun to be found in the business was pulling off deals in the cocoa-bean and sugar markets, stocking up on reserves when prices dropped and laying off when prices rose. Then in 1915 Hershey's wife, whom he always called Kitty, died—of a long illness never described in any material written anywhere about the family. This no doubt made the Hershey scene somewhat painful to its founder, and in 1917 he took his mother down to Havana for a long stay. There he learned to smoke Corona-Coronas and to bet on the horses at the track. His mother, now eighty, found out that sugar was grown in Cuba and suggested to her son that he put up his own sugar mill so he could save money in supplying the plant back home. The upshot was a typical Hershey production on a big scale—an entire sugar-mill town called Central Hershey. Twenty-eight miles from Havana, it boasted, besides a mill that started out with a capacity of a hundred million pounds of sugar a year, a hotel, a baseball field, a golf course, a park, and a passenger and freight railroad that connected the sixty-thousand-acre estate with Havana in one direction and Matanzas in the other. Soon Hershey was raising hothouse orchids as well as prize Plymouth Rock chickens, and he bought a ten-thousand-dollar bull to sire a herd of Holstein dairy cattle. He built a hundred fifty houses for employees, hired doctors and dentists for them, and bought them an ocean beach—eventually there were several thousand men working for Hershey in various Cuban operations, including five other sugar mills added later. The topper came when Hershey, taking in a group of children whose parents were all suddenly killed in a bloody Cuban train wreck (not on Hershey's line), founded another orphans' school. Within a few years the citizens of nearby Matanzas, originally suspicious of Hershey's motives, had made him an adopted son and honorary citizen.

Except for a single setback, when he lost two and a half million in the sugar market in 1920, Hershey increased his sales and profits every year. In 1927 the company issued new shares on the New York Stock Exchange, but the school retained ownership of two-thirds of the business, as it does today. When Prohibition killed the beer trade, Schlitz, in Milwaukee, made a heavy and frightening bid to take over the chocolate-bar business, but Hershey stood firm and survived. Hershey also protested a candy tax on chocolate on the ground that chocolate is a food, not a candy, and took the case to the Supreme Court, where it was astutely decided that food or candy, whatever chocolate was, it was meant to be included in the taxation. A gang of six brothers named Hershey began putting out chocolates under the brand name Hershey Brothers but were stopped when Milton Hershey sued them. By 1929 the peaceful town of Hershey was producing forty-two million dollars' worth of chocolate a year, and Milton S. Hershey's original vision was pretty close to his idea of how it ought to be: "an industrial utopia where the things of modern progress all center in a town that has no poverty, no nuisances, and no evil."

He wanted to make things nice for everybody. He suggested that his department store be turned into a co-op, owned by his employees, but the wives were suspicious, fearing they would not be able to shop anywhere else, so he dropped the idea. Sam Rosenberger also recalls a short-lived profit-sharing plan in which workers could get stock in the firm as part of their pay. But many workers, with the spirit of the Plain People strong in their families, believed that dealing in stock was sinful. "It's a type of gambling," Rosenberger explains today. "My parents did not approve of it." A pension plan was also put before a committee of employees for their consideration, but when they failed to agree on how it should be set up, Hershey lost patience with them and dropped the idea.

Hershey's Shangri-la amazingly did keep the outside world at bay when the Depression hit the country in 1929. Chocolate sales dropped some, but cocoa-bean prices fell even more, and there were a lot of Americans who could still afford a nickel Hershey bar for lunch. So in 1930 the firm made an amazing seven and a half million dollars'

profit. But what saved Hershey people from the effects of the nationwide slump was Milton Hershey's enthusiastic local counterattack: he immediately started a huge building-construction program that would have done credit to a good-sized city, with the idea of keeping his people at work. He could fulfill some of his old utopian projects and at the same time take advantage of dropping prices of construction materials.

His mother, who died in 1920, had always kept him from realizing one big dream. For many years, up on Pat's Hill north of town, he had kept a grove of evergreens around a great bald spot meant for an imposing resort to be called Hotel Hershey. Now he showed architects post cards of hotels he had visited in Egypt and Spain, and the result was a Hollywoodish castle of a hundred fifty rooms, with an indoor courtyard sporting a blue ceiling with clouds and green-carpet grass between pathways. A great circular dining room posed engineering problems because Hershey, who had been stashed at tables behind pillars in some of the European restaurants, insisted there be no posts at all in his place. (In his Cuba hotel he had had a private dining room built for himself when he found that his Cuban customers played a radio very loudly in the public restaurant there.) When the hotel was nearly finished, Hershey brought over sixty families of Italian workmen to lay tile, and Lowell Thomas rotundly pronounced the result "a palace that out-palaces the palaces of the maharajahs of India."

At the same time that the hotel was going up, at a cost of a million and a half, a sprawling five-story community center was also being built, across from the factory, to cost twice as much as the hotel. Its rooms decorated in variously clashing Italian Renaissance and French provincial styles, it has a library, a swimming pool, fencing and boxing gyms, a dining hall, a dormitory, and two theatres, one for plays and the other for movies (Hershey, who was somewhat prudish, had these censored for many years for "sensual dances"). Hershey also built new schools, both for the town and for his orphan boys, who by the late thirties numbered well over a thousand; and he put up a sports arena with a novel roof of reinforced concrete for his hockey team, the Hershey Bears (commonly called Hershey Bars by local boosters). He tried to talk the five local churches into letting him build them all one great big church that they would use in turn, and when he found everybody sour on his idea, he gave each church twenty thousand dollars to fix up its old buildings. He built a new stadium seating sixteen thousand, and he claimed: "No man in Hershey was dropped by reason of the depression." As a sort of Christmas-stocking stuffer, Hershey also gave away his home, High Point, to be used as a country club by his employees, keeping a couple of upstairs rooms for his own residence, and he hung an inscribed plaque above his fireplace reading "My Home I Give To You—The Best I Have."

For his executives Hershey put another small fortune into a new office building constructed without windows to be very, very modern; and coincidentally it kept out the

Opposite, top: busy Hershey, Pa., in 1913, when trainloads of sightseers —like those at left—visited the town. The main factory, still extant, is in the background. Below are apartments for employees, built in the 1930's, and Hershey Park with its miniature railroad. The resplendent Hotel Hershey, above, was opened in 1933 to provide for the yearly deluge of tourists.

The benefactor and one of his wards, a lad from the orphanage Hershey founded

"chockle shtink." But no sooner had the Depression been survived than there appeared an unbelievable sight right outside this new structure, and smack in front of the marvellous new community center: union organizers, picketing! At seventy-nine Hershey had made his utopia, had brought it through the Depression unscathed and unchanged, and his people obviously loved him for it. A friend said that when he saw the pickets, he was "like a kid who's had his face slapped." Employees were given a twelve-cent raise, to sixty cents an hour, but the union men stayed. This was in March, 1937. A month later, when seasonal layoffs put some recently hired workers out of jobs, the union claimed its members were being discriminated against (company practice had traditionally been to lay off employees, when necessary, from among those living beyond a five-mile radius of the plant).

On April 2 twelve hundred workers closed down the plant with a sit-down strike. They left the next day, then occupied the plant again on April 6. The closing of the plant meant that eight hundred thousand pounds of milk arriving in Hershey daily had no market. Local farmers were losing ten thousand dollars a day. Five thousand marchers, including several hundred nonunion Hershey workers and a lot of angry farmers, paraded in the nearby

When he set up the orphanage in 1909, Hershey intended it to be a vocational school for young boys. No girls were, or are now, enrolled. Here it is in 1912, with George Copenhaver, the first superintendent, posing with a group of fifteen chocolate-workers-to-be.

town of Palmyra by torchlight that night, accompanied by local fire trucks, the Hershey Drum and Bugle Corps, the Boy Scouts, and the American Legion. "Hershey's in America, Let's Keep It Here" read one banner. The letters CIO were spelled out: "Communistic Idiot Outlaws." The farmers and independent workers held a big meeting in the sports arena the next day as strikers ran up the CIO flag on a pole on the factory roof—above the Stars and Stripes. The farmers gave the strikers an ultimatum—out of the plant by 1 P.M.—and then marched on the factory. In spite of a week of continuous tension there were no police on the scene. At the last moment the strikers decided to give up, but it was too late—there was no stopping the angry crowd, armed with whips, iron pipe, baseball bats, axe handles, rubber hose, ice picks, and carving knives. They forced their way inside—a union man accused a company executive of unlocking the main entrance for them from the inside—and beat and shoved the strikers outside to run a long gauntlet of two rows of farmers and independents who struck and slashed at them and kicked them on their way past.

"The frightened strikers ran all the harder," reported the *New York Times*, "pulling coats and shirts over their heads. Many collapsed, with blood streaming from swollen faces and misshapen noses. At the end of the block-long line they were searched. Then they sprinted for freedom and for hiding places. The former attackers now formed stretcher squads and helped the most battered of their enemies to waiting automobiles for the short trip to Hershey Hospital. The two strike leaders, Russell Behman and John Loy, were not let off quite so easily. They were taken over to a spacious section of the lawn fronting the factory and were subjected to a two-fisted drubbing which left them quite exhausted." Later Loy blamed Hershey president Murrie for failing to call off the crowd; the governor blamed the local sheriff for letting the mob move in with no police hindrance whatever. Final count was about fifty wounded, two seriously from ice picks shoved into their stomachs. As for Hershey, the old man himself had watched the farmers marching on his factory, and a reporter wrote: "As they passed by singing, tears streamed from his eyes, but he did not speak."

"It was never the same in Hershey after that," Sam Rosenberger says now. "Before, people were more like a big family." The battle split the community; a *Times* reporter had noted that "one of the chief interests . . . is trying to find where one's neighbors stand in the dispute. The newspaper photographs of the mêlée are very useful

The rude shock for paternalistic Hershey came in 1937. As he watched, loyal workers joined angry farmers with no outlet for their milk in storming his plant to evict sit-down strikers inside. "It was never the same in Hershey after that," a former worker said.

U.P.I.

in this connection." Ray Carlucetti, the present business manager of Local 464, Chocolate Workers, says that scars are still not quite healed and that among older union members now, "If you find one who is really all out gung-ho for the union, you can guess maybe he was a scab back in those days." After the beatings the strike faltered, with a few attempts at picketing by the CIO while the independents handed out handbills reading "Sit-down is a strike against orphan boys." In his first interview in fourteen years Hershey blamed the strike on "foolish radicals."

"Four or five of them simply misled a small minority of the employes into this strike," Hershey told Robert S. Bird of the *Times*. "I know that many of these strikers are people I brought here during the depression years. I made work for them during the depression. There was no depression in Hershey. I know the chocolate business all the way through, and I am not sure that some union leaders who would tell me how to run the chocolate business know very much about it." Hershey said he thought that a union was not necessary to his employees' welfare. "Of course," he said, "I know the answer that will be made to that statement. Old man Hershey has got something up his sleeve. People said that around here thirty years ago when I wanted to start a co-operative store. Well, I gave up the idea. I had a band around here about that time and I decided to help them out by giving them a hall rent free. I even let them put in a candy and a tobacco counter to help swell their profits. But I found after a great Fourth of July celebration that they still had no money in the till. They had a turnout of people that should have given them a good profit, but they had no profit, and they did not know why. They had smoked up the cigars and cigarettes and drank the pop themselves. The co-operative idea didn't work and I decided to take over the business end of it myself."

Two weeks after the battle Hershey workers voted 1,542 to 781 for an independent union, the Independent Chocolate Workers. (The CIO accused it of being a company union, and two years later the National Labor Relations Board upheld this position, finally bringing the CIO officially into Hershey.) Peace was restored in Hershey, but bitterness remained below the surface sweetness, visible even through the rigorous cheeriness of a surprise party for Milton Hershey's eightieth birthday, the crowning moment of his life, five months after the bloody strike. While some seven thousand people sat silent in the sports arena a friend lured Hershey inside, pretending he wanted him to examine some new lights. Hershey emerged onto a platform to find the throng cheering, applauding, and blowing tin horns and ringing handbells in his honor. They sang "Happy Birthday," and they wept, and they cheered Hershey's huge cake with the eighty electric candles. In one of his rare public speeches Hershey thanked them, saying, "I've tried to make things pleasant and agreeable for everybody, although, as you know, some people have been telling you otherwise. They've been telling you that I am a grasping old fellow whose only purpose in life is to grab everything he sees." There followed a minister's half-hour eulogy of the town's founder and then five vaudeville acts and a dance.

The disappointment Hershey felt in what he thought of as the ingratitude of his workers stayed with him, and there was a touch of sourness in the last years of his life. One Christmas Eve a cousin found him alone in his rooms, complaining of having no family. The cousin reminded him of all the orphan boys, but Hershey, who never had had any children, refused to be cheered. "They are not my own," he said. In his last years he became careless of his usual neat dress, but he was still lively. His doctor writes that his nurse would drive him around, and "if anything caught his eye they'd stop for a closer look. One day he crawled under a fence to see something in a field. The nurse turned away for a moment and when she looked again he had disappeared. She found him. He had fallen into a sink hole and she had to haul him out." A few weeks before his death, at eighty-eight, he was experimenting in his rooms with new formulas for cocoa-butter soap. Then a sudden cold sent him to the hospital, where, on October 13, 1945, he died of heart failure.

But the company, now called the Hershey Foods Corporation, lives on. In 1971 it reported sales of over four hundred million dollars and a twenty-million-dollar profit, of which 90 per cent came from chocolate and cocoa; new subsidiaries making spaghetti and restaurant equipment accounted for the rest. The old nickel Hershey bar is gone—it lasted from 1903 to 1970, and in just the years since the last war it shrank twelve times, until it nearly disappeared.* (The surviving dime bar now weighs a bit over an ounce.) In the 1960's new plants were opened in California and in Canada, not without certain problems. According to a 1970 report in the *Wall Street Journal*, there was trouble making the chocolate taste right. For a time Pennsylvania milk was shipped to Canada to try to improve the flavor, but it didn't help. Things have gone better in California, but some say the best Hershey bars still come from Hershey.

Current president Harold S. Mohler, a cautiously affable, round-faced, cigar-smoking engineer, feels the main difference around Hershey over the years is that "people aren't work-oriented the way they used to be. I don't mean they won't work or don't like to work, it's just that work doesn't take up all their waking hours the way it

*The public relations department of Hershey Foods points out that the size of the chocolate bar is kept in proportion to costs and therefore fluctuates: several times since 1945 the bar has temporarily *increased* in size.

used to be. And the community is more cosmopolitan now; not so high a percentage of the people work for Hershey now." Another prominent Hershey executive, board chairman William E. Schiller, who has an ambassadorial stance and a very direct eye, says the firm wants to broaden itself into the specialty-foods field—"but we are not hell-bent on acquiring new subsidiaries. We want to work gradually into the market created by people who eat away from home. But chocolate will remain our main concern." Of the community Schiller says emphatically: "People here are really great. It's a wonderful place to raise children." Like most Hershey employees, Schiller eats a lot of free chocolate—unwrapped, it is available anywhere in the plant, but you're not supposed to take it home with you. "I don't see how anyone can get tired of chocolate," says Schiller.

As far as the chocolate business in Hershey is concerned, the only major change since the founder's days—except maybe the attitudes of the workers—has been the advent of national advertising. For decades Hershey's cavalier refusal to advertise had rankled admen everywhere, for obviously his success seemed to prove that it did not, after all, necessarily pay to advertise. In fact Hershey did indulge in certain kinds of advertising, but not the kind that used advertising agencies. His name was printed large in silver letters on his wrappers, so that wherever they might fall, they became an effective ad in themselves—Hershey was said always to have kicked them right side up with his toe when he saw them in a gutter. Before World War I Hershey bars had post cards inside the wrapper illustrating such milk-chocolate themes as a cocoa pod or a herd of cows in a meadow, and over the years advertising copy has been prepared for use by retailers. Although all this was a far cry from the usual advertising programs of national corporations, the New York Sunday *News* not long ago gave Hershey special credit: "Hershey ran what was undoubtedly the most costly long-term promotional campaign in history—the community of Hershey itself." One deep thinker in the advertising field believes Hershey had automatically good sales luck because of the pleonasm of his name—the repeated meaning, or double feminine, of *her* and *she*.

But it wasn't until 1970 that the first Hershey television commercials surprised the advertising fraternity. One such precious minute shows a herd of angry cows charging down the main street of Jefferson City, Missouri, because they have heard that the local children are not drinking their milk. Following the cows are some jeeps loaded with Hershey Instant. Describing the dénouement, a *New York Times* advertising columnist wrote: "The kids, bowing to this show of force and flavor, drink their milk. The cows leave udderly victorious."

The Hershey firm, among businessmen, has a reputation for stodginess. A Wall Street broker explains, "When your company has to feed, clothe, house and educate 1,500 orphans every year, you just have to be conservative." Nevertheless, the company is putting out a new chocolate and peanut item called the Rally bar, and chairman Schiller recklessly promises, "I personally will eat every one of these we don't sell." The orphanage has, in fact, accrued so much money it doesn't know quite how to spend it, and recently it had to get special legal permission to give away fifty million dollars for a new medical center for Pennsylvania State University. The school already has treated itself to a massive Founder's Hall that looks like a recently added attraction to the Strip in Las Vegas; a huge mosaic set in its floor illustrates "twelve significant events in the life of our founder." The resort-like poshness everywhere in the school is defended by its president on the ground that "if a boy is presented with a bright, clean wall, he won't make a mark on it."

But some of the union members would like some of that bright, clean wall for themselves. They do not want it given to them; they'll settle for the cash and make one of their own. Ray Carlucetti, the union business manager, admits that the current average pay of $3.80 an hour is near the top of the chocolate industry, but this fact still does not stop the undercurrents of restiveness that began back in 1937 and that most recently broke out in a wildcat strike of three thousand workers on June 17, 1972. At midnight a mob that reminded old-timers of the pioneer CIO strikers stoned passing cars, threw nails on streets, and beat up two nonunion workers, college students with temporary jobs whose cars were smashed up for good measure. The students were released from the hospital after treatment for cuts, bruises, and sprains, but for a time it looked as if the spirit of the old CIO had been ghosted back into Hershey to settle the old score. After sixty state policemen broke up the riot, the protesters, who were disputing factory rules on work breaks, agreed to arbitrate the matter. Carlucetti, who did not condone the demonstration, points out that the workers for years have had all this wealth paraded before them, in the town and out at the school, and they feel it is about time they got their hands on some of it, too. They do, of course, still get the traditional Christmas turkey from the company.

When Hershey died, a New York *Herald Tribune* editorialist commented, "Was it not at bottom a despotism, no matter how benevolent and practical? The entire scheme was enlightened, intelligent and permeated with a rare human decency. And yet . . . it was a sort of feudalism." It was a fair enough epitaph.

Roy Bongartz, a former member of the staff of The New Yorker, *is a free-lance writer who specializes in stories about unusual American communities and is currently working on a book on that subject.*

Reading, Writing, and History

At one point in her journalistic career Dorothy Thompson, learning of a proposed magazine piece on her life, wrote: "I wish someone would present me as a female. . . . [It's] heresy which the feminists wouldn't like, but . . . I'd throw the state of the nation into the ashcan for anyone I loved."

It was not a wholly truthful statement, but an exasperated reaction to the dilemma of a successful woman who always had to face the direct or hinted accusation that competence outside the home was unfeminine. Anne Royall, born 124 years before Dorothy—and likewise a successful writer on topics of the day—once felt compelled in similar fashion to disown fellowship with feminists who downgraded the traditional interests and allurements of their sex. Condemning Amelia Bloomer's emancipated costume of a loose smock over baggy trousers, she asked: "Do our sisters intend to part with their last and best treasure—modesty . . . the sweet rounding waist, the unspeakable charm of a swelling bosom?" Yet sweetness, modesty, and charm were never attributes of Anne Royall's.

Both women, in their careers, offer food for reflection on the changing and changeless elements in woman-

ANNE ROYALL'S U.S.A.
by Bessie Rowland James.
Rutgers University Press,
447 pp. $15.00

DOROTHY THOMPSON:
A Legend in Her Time
by Marion K. Sanders.
Houghton Mifflin Co., 432 pp. $10.00

hood and journalism in the United States. Both are the subjects of lively new biographies.

Anne Royall was born (as Anne Newport) in 1769 and was raised on the Pennsylvania frontier. She was often within earshot of Indian war whoops and had lost both a father and a stepfather by the time she was fourteen. She suffered the humiliation of being "domestic help" for a time but was rescued when her employer, Colonel William Royall, took her to be his woman and later his wife. Royall, a Revolutionary War veteran, was a Virginia planter who had gone west to make his fortune—an objective he never achieved, thanks to an absorption in books and brandy. When he died in 1812, he left his widow a modest subsistence. But relatives who had always resented his

lower-class bride successfully sued to break the will.

In her fifties by then—quite old for that era—Anne Royall had to support herself. Frontier energy and self-reliance came to her aid. She had a knack for pungent pen sketches in her letters, and she now moved to Alabama (a brand-new state then, largely wilderness), wrote a number of accounts of people and places there, and then began the tedious task of travelling from town to town soliciting subscriptions that would pay for putting the reports into book form. By the time the volume emerged, she had settled in Washington to lobby for a pension as an ex-soldier's widow.

The *Letters from Alabama* were a scandalous success. Anne had, with country-girl bluntness, described the fluid, yeasty society she found just as it was—full of hornswogglers and hypocrites as well as heroes. She got a reputation best summarized by John Quincy Adams: "Stripped of all her sex's delicacy, but unable to forfeit its privilege of gentle treatment . . . she goes about like a virago errant in enchanted armor." (Adams, however, was relatively friendly to her—though biographer Bessie James finds no truth in the story that Anne

By BERNARD A. WEISBERGER

once got an interview with him by surprising him during his morning naked swim in the Potomac and sitting on his clothes.)

From 1830 onward Anne continued to travel and to write, not sparing her enemies, among them evangelical preachers, anti-Masons, and all pompous males. Her enemies in turn paid no particular heed to her alleged woman's "privilege of gentle treatment." One Yankee defender of revealed religion threw her down a flight of porch steps (breaking her leg); a Pittsburgh bookstore clerk horsewhipped her—when she was nearly seventy!—and she was tried in Washington as a "common scold" and convicted (two reporters paid her fine as a gesture on behalf of a free press).

She founded two successive newspapers, *Paul Pry* in 1831 and *The Huntress* in 1836, each a compact package of powdered gall. She lived until 1854 —time enough to see her America span the continent and to be alarmed by sectional "fanatics" who would tear the nation apart. At her death she was eulogized by a local journal as a woman of "considerable literary attainments . . . and of strict integrity," a description honorable enough for any member of the working press.

Dorothy Thompson was born the daughter of a Methodist minister in 1893, spent her childhood in upstate New York parsonages, and was graduated from Syracuse University in 1914. As a proper "new woman" of the day she was mildly interested in social work and female suffrage. As a girl of unusual intelligence and vitality she was passionately interested in the great world around her and in lively and articulate people who either ran it or described it with style. In 1920, after holding various public-relations jobs, she went to Europe in flight from a painful crush on a married man. Armed with letters of introduction, she soon numbered labor leaders, journalists, artists, and politicians among her friends. They were the top layer of a European society

politically and economically ruined by war but full of intellectual ferment.

Soon she found a base in Vienna and a job as a foreign correspondent for the Philadelphia *Public Ledger*. She rejoiced in liberation from small-town Methodism's patterns of conduct, but she lost none of its moralistic zeal. She enjoyed liquor, late hours, keen companions, and romances in Paris, London, Vienna, and Berlin—and wrote dispatches that were tense, imaginative, and deeply committed to exposing the perils surrounding European democracies. In a day of great foreign correspondents—Duranty, Gunther, Sheean, Shirer—she held her own.

In the late 1920's she returned to the United States to "settle down" as the wife of Sinclair Lewis—a second marriage for both, which ended in divorce in 1942. It was then that she came into her own as a regular columnist for the New York *Herald Tribune*, as well as a prolific lecturer, magazine contributor, and radio commentator. What made her noteworthy and notorious was her untiring and stormy anti-Fascism. (Hitler had thrown her out of Germany in 1934 for her unflattering reporting of Nazi ways and works.) Many of us who were her readers in those days still remember her flaming warnings, to an America still dreaming of isolation and security behind ocean "barriers," that a world dominated by Fascist bullies would be a nightmare of insecurity for us all. Her vigorous interventionism, violent castigation of opponents, occasional streaks of pontifical self-righteousness—all made her numerous enemies. But like other controversial figures of that stormy era (John L. Lewis, Fiorello La Guardia, or F.D.R. himself), she scorned impartiality when convinced that she had truth on her side.

The postwar years brought both comforts and the inevitable sadnesses of old age. Unlike poor Anne Royall, Dorothy Thompson was a financial

success whose generous earnings sustained a pleasant life-style. But friends and followers tended to fade away as a new generation, indifferent to its elders' battles, emerged. When she died of a heart attack in 1961, many had forgotten her—and those who remembered shared mixed impressions of her as a woman courageous and shrill, generous and petulant, sophisticated and rigid—a collection of turbulent contradictions, all well illustrated in Marion Sanders' story.

Yet both ladies, stormy critics that they were, illustrate a point. Faultfinding is a basic attribute of American journalism—ever since the first newspaper here, Boston's *Publick Occurrences,* was suppressed after one issue in 1690 because editor Benjamin Harris had made "Reflections of a very high nature" on the authorities. Anne Royall awakened her countrymen to their own vast potential and raw energies, often outraging them in the process by querulous observations. Dorothy Thompson was one of a generation of newspapermen (and women) who aroused the United States, early in the twentieth century, to the unavoidable responsibilities of strength in a shrinking world. The audience often cared little for the message or the tone of its deliverers.

History has given us this kind of contentious and faultfinding press as both our burden and our advantage. For a responsible press is one that will goad and pry—and our best-known press workers have often had brassy personalities, strong appetites for drink and dispute, and erratic domestic lives. The public hardly admires men with these characteristics and is shocked out of its wits by women with them. Yet the nation owes some gratitude to these unhonored prophets, and perhaps a special debt to women in the field, who are twice alienated from the comforts of conformity: they are neither average citizens nor average women. ☆

FATHER COUGHLIN

The following letter comes to us from Dr. Sheldon Marcus, chairman of the Division of Urban Education, School of Education, Fordham University, who is the author of *Father Coughlin: The Tumultuous Life of the Priest of the Little Flower,* which will soon be published by Little, Brown and Company.

I read with interest Robert S. Gallagher's interview with Father Charles E. Coughlin in the October, 1972, issue of AMERICAN HERITAGE. Unfortunately, the article contained some misinformation.

First of all, Mr. Gallagher claimed that his interview with Father Coughlin was the first one given in the past three decades in which the priest discussed his career. Since Father Coughlin's demise as a controversial public figure in 1942, he has periodically given interviews to newsmen. I myself was able to secure interviews with him in 1970 which proved valuable in helping me write his biography.

The explanation Coughlin gave Mr. Gallagher of having church support for his activities is misleading. In 1937 the Vatican, believing that Coughlin was effective in combating the spread of communism in the United States, intervened on his behalf when his new superior, Archbishop Edward Mooney, attempted to silence him. This intervention enabled Coughlin to embark on the most vitriolic and controversial phase of his public life, which lasted until Eugenio Cardinal Pacelli, who had rebuked Coughlin for his activities during the 1936 Presidential elections, became pope in 1939, at which time the Vatican withdrew its support.

From reading the article one would gather that Father Coughlin and Franklin Roosevelt were close friends and that Coughlin's criticism of F.D.R. was based on a disagreement over monetary policy. According to what he told me, Coughlin's split with Roosevelt was predicated on his belief that the President had merely used him in the effort to attract the priest's supporters to the New Deal. Coughlin told me that "he [Roosevelt] owed me things. After all, I helped make him President. We were supposed to be partners. He said he would rely on me . . . that I would be an important advisor. But he was a liar. He never took my advice. He just used me." Coughlin never understood that Roosevelt, as a consummate politician, was doing everything possible to perform the prime function of a political candidate—winning elections.

When Coughlin realized that he was merely one of many who could talk to the President, his feeling of betrayal surfaced and took the form of vituperative criticism of the President, criticism which increased in intensity after the 1936 Presidential election, in which his Union Party ticket was soundly defeated.

In addition, in the article Father Coughlin said that he had to speak out on the critical issues of the day because of his concern for social justice. Coughlin's private actions were, however, at considerable variance from his public utterances. He denounced bankers and Wall Street machinations, yet he was a large silver speculator, invested heavily in the stock market, and boasted of his friendship with the most influential bankers in the Detroit area, who, he claims, still constantly seek his advice on fiscal matters. He denounced those who grew rich from speculative and business ventures, but he himself became wealthy and today still lives in one of the most exclusive areas of suburban Detroit.

In Mr. Gallagher's interview Father Coughlin states that he was neither anti-Semitic nor pro-Hitler. Yet Coughlin admits that he reprinted the anti-Semitic forgeries the *Protocols of the Elders of Zion,* although he told Gallagher that "I couldn't prove they're false, I couldn't prove they're genuine. . . . " Coughlin did not ask "Zionists" to disavow the *Protocols,* as the interview stated. Zionists were not an issue in the United States in the 1930's. Instead he asked "good Jews" to disavow the *Protocols.*

Apparently Coughlin has also forgotten that he not only lauded Hitler as a foe of communism and as an individual who had solved the economic problems of the depression but that he hoped for a German victory over England and the Soviet Union. Stories of German atrocities against Jews were dismissed as Jewish propaganda in his weekly, *Social Justice.*

In a time of great frustration, Father Coughlin spawned discord, hate, and violence. What made his pronouncements even more dangerous was that his diatribes were delivered under the guise of religion and piety. He was a man of the cloth, but he stands as an illustration of how bigotry can emanate from religion.

Our author and contributing editor, Mr. Gallagher, replies:

The factual content of all quotations in the "Before the Colors Fade" series is carefully checked; the opinions, recollections, and personal judgments represent the views of the person interviewed, which is, of course, the basic purpose of any oral-history project. In 1966, when he retired from the pulpit of the Shrine of the Little Flower, Father Coughlin told a network television correspondent that he was still not at liberty to talk about his controversial activities. At the conclusion of my interviews with him in May, 1972, Coughlin said that this was the first time he had ever discussed his career in depth for publication.

ON THE WRONG TRACK

A number of alert readers have called our attention to real or supposed errors in our captions for the trolley-car post cards that appeared in the February, 1973, issue. Mr. Benjamin R. Jordan of California tells us that in our picture on page 32 we have "placed the Rubio Canyon in Griffith Park instead of its proper location on the north slope of the San Gabriel Valley, a slip of some eleven miles as the crow flies, and a little farther by street car." Mr. Jordan, however, graciously provides us with a couple of excuses: "Los Angeles' several earthquakes could have brought the two locations together and replaced them again. Besides, with the ever-present smog permeating the area, I don't think that anyone is really sure just where the two places are in relation to each other anyway." We came out better on a complaint by Mr. D. Douglas of San Francisco, who wrote "in sorrow more than anger" to urge us to fire the caption writer who identified the street railway on the back cover as a trolley rather than a cable car. The lack of overhead wires does indeed suggest a cable car, and in fact the lines on Pennsylvania Avenue were originally powered by moving cables. But by the early years of this century, when the picture was taken, the city had shifted over to electric power. So those are trolleys in the picture, fizzing along by the grace of an electric shoe held against the underground wires. Finally, we would like to apologize for omitting El Paso's international car line to Juarez, Mexico, from our list of working electric trolleys in America. At the time the issue went to press, the line was out of service while repairs were being made. Happily, it's now running again, and travellers can ride over the border and back on the only international streetcar line in North America.

PIECES OF KING

We are pleased to report that last year an antiques dealer named Louis Miller, armed with a seventy-dollar metal detector and information from an article in our August, 1958, issue entitled "The Search for the Missing King," dug up a long-buried fragment of the most famous statue in early American history.

Five days after the signing of the Declaration of Independence a courier from Philadelphia galloped into New York bearing the news that the colonists there were now part of the embattled United States of America. A defiant citizenry converged on Bowling Green and gathered around the huge gilded-lead equestrian statue of King George III that had been erected there six years before. The patriots threw ropes around the likeness of their sometime monarch and toppled it to the ground. The statue was chopped into pieces, and two tons of these were shipped off to Litchfield, Connecticut, to be melted down for bullets. But not all of the king was fired at his troops, and from time to time fragments of the statue turned up. The last of these, a group of four large pieces including the tail of the horse, came to light more than a hundred years ago.

Louis Miller, however, was undismayed by the century-long lack of new fragments and occasionally went prospecting for parts of the statue along the route followed so long ago. Miller's search paid off last October when he was prowling through swampy ground two miles from his Wilton, Connecticut, home. His metal detector started the electronic keening that meant it had picked up some metallic substance buried in the soil. Miller dug down and came up with a twenty-pound piece of lead that is unquestionably part of the two-hundred-year-old statue—although which part is not clear. At the present time the fragment is on display in the Museum of the City of New York, and the Connecticut treasure hunter is planning new forays with better equipment.

MISFIRE

We regret neglecting to credit the Historical Society of York County, Pennsylvania, in our portfolio on the Kentucky rifle (February, 1973). This excellent institution was sponsor and co-publisher of the book from which our excerpt was taken.

IN GILBERT'S BARN

WILLIAM R. RAY

The patent models in our portfolio beginning on page 49 of this issue are only a minute fraction of the tens of thousands that still survive. O. Rundle Gilbert, the owner of most of them, is shown here in one of his barns, surrounded by ranks and stacks of the models that he has recently unpacked. Somewhere nearby are hundreds of unopened crates, all filled with patent models. We can only guess at what treasures from America's technological infancy are yet to come to light.

WHOSE FAULT WAS IT?

Every schoolchild knows that the Liberty Bell is cracked; the crack is almost as famous as the bell itself. But just when and why the crack appeared is a much more esoteric matter. It is sometimes assumed, patriotically but mistakenly, that the bell cracked out of overenthusiasm while being rung to celebrate the Declaration of Independence in 1776. Somewhat more solid evidence suggests that it broke in 1835, either in July while tolling a knell for Chief Justice John Marshall or on Washington's Birthday, when a group of small boys pulled too energetically on the rope. One of the boys, Emmanuel Rauch, was interviewed in 1911 and stuck to that story, observing besides that for any funeral the bell's clapper would have been muffled and unlikely to cause damage. In 1846 an attempt was made to put the great bell in ringing order by drilling out the edges of the crack to prevent their rubbing together. This worked about as well as the dentistry characteristic of the period; and when the bell was rung on February 23 of that year (Washington's Birthday having fallen on Sunday), the crack suddenly split open farther. Since then the only sound heard from the Liberty Bell has been a disappointing thunk created by tapping it gently with a small mallet on triumphant occasions like the Allied invasion of Normandy in 1944.

But *why* did the bell crack in the first place? This highly technical question has recently been given extensive study by a professional metallurgist, Dr. Alan R. Rosenfield, an expert on metal fracture

who is associated with the Battelle Memorial Institute in Columbus, Ohio. He has come up with some interesting facts and explanations. In general, he points out, "bells are necessarily made out of brittle metal, and they often break. Even Big Ben is slightly cracked."

The Liberty Bell is a moderately large one, with a lip circumference of twelve feet and a total weight of over a ton. In 1751, when the Assembly of the Province of Pennsylvania wanted a suitable bell for the newly completed belfry of their State House in Philadelphia, they ordered one from the Whitechapel Bell Foundry in London—presumably because they did not trust any foundry in America to design such a large bell. It arrived at Philadelphia in the late summer of 1752. To everyone's surprise and dismay it promptly cracked "by a stroke of the clapper without any other violence, as it was hung up to try the sound."

To save a round trip to England two local foundrymen—John Pass and John Stow—were engaged to recast the bell. While they do not appear to have been experienced bell founders, they knew that the ideal bronze alloy for a large bell should contain about 77 per cent copper and 23 per cent tin. They also knew that an increase in the proportion of tin improves the tone and resonance of a bell—one might say its tintinnabulation—but makes it more brittle. They therefore reasoned that their bell, as received from England, probably contained too much tin. With that in mind they made a mold from the original bell to preserve the design, melted down the metal, added one and a half ounces of copper per pound of bronze, and recast. The bell that resulted, however, was judged to have poor tone, and they allegedly tried again—this time adding about one-fourth per cent silver in order to sweeten the tone. ("This," comments Dr. Rosenfield, "reminds one of the story that the Great Bell of Peking owes its sweet tone to the sacrifice of a maiden who jumped into the molten bronze. Silver does little or nothing to improve the resonance of bell metal, nor do maidens.") When Pass and Stow's second attempt came out of the mold, it was deemed acceptable if not altogether satisfactory, and it was hung in the State House belfry —its destiny as America's Liberty Bell, of course, undreamed of.

Pass and Stow, perhaps sensing that this was their one chance for renown, added their signature to the bell in raised letters no less prominent than those used for the inscription around the crown: PASS AND STOW / PHILADᴬ / MDCCLIII. The crown inscription, chosen when the bell was originally ordered from England, reads: PROCLAIM LIBERTY THROUGHOUT

ALL THE LAND UNTO ALL THE INHABITANTS THEREOF LEV[iticus]. XXV Vᵴx./BY ORDER OF THE ASSEMBLY OF THE PROVINCE OF PENSYLVANIA FOR THE STATE HOUSE IN PHILADᴬ This, including the misspelling of Pennsylvania, presumably was reproduced by the mold just as it had appeared on the original bell. Without the inscription, clearly, the bell would never have been adopted by the American people as a prime symbol of the Revolution. As a matter of fact, this was slow in coming: the bell was not commonly known as the Liberty Bell until the 1840's and in 1828 it was even offered for sale by the City of Philadelphia as salvage. (It was refused because it was thought too expensive to move.)

But back to the crack. Dr. Rosenfield points out that, quite aside from orthography, there were both visible and invisible defects in the bell. Pass and Stow were not skillful enough to produce a bell with a uniformly smooth surface: there are numerous pockmarks and some seams. Moreover, modern metallurgical analysis of a small sample has indicated two defects in the metal itself: it still has too much tin (24 per cent by weight), and it contains many nonmetallic impurities, globs of lead, and small voids. Any one of these irregularities, or a combination of them, could have started the fatal crack under the impact of the bell's clapper.

On top of this, the Liberty Bell had a rough time during the Revolution: when the British approached Philadelphia in 1777, it was loaded on a wagon and jolted over bad roads to Allentown for safekeeping until 1778. It is said to have been dropped at least once en route, which may have produced an incipient, microscopic crack. Finally. any big bell is subject to metal fatigue—the gradual deterioration of part of the bell under a repeated number of strikings; and the Liberty Bell's structural defects may have led to a fatigue crack some time in its first fifty or sixty years of existence. This would not have impaired the tone of the bell until the crack reached a critical size and then fractured rapidly and catastrophically, as apparently it did in 1835. Alternatively, a single overload—an extraheavy blow from the clapper—could have fractured the bell all at once.

Could the Liberty Bell be melted down and recast so that it could ring again? Certainly, our expert says; and in fact the Whitechapel Bell Foundry, still in business in London, offered to do just that in 1945. The offer was politely turned down by the federal government. The crack, it would seem, has become as sacred as the bell itself, and to remove it would be like subjecting the honorable battle scars of an old soldier to plastic surgery.   —*E.M.H.*